THE STALIN REVOLUTION

Fulfillment or Betrayal of Communism?

PROBLEMS IN EUROPEAN CIVILIZATION

UNDER THE EDITORIAL DIRECTION OF
Ralph W. Greenlaw* and Dwight E. Lee†

Other volumes in preparation

PROBLEMS IN EUROPEAN CIVILIZATION

THE
STALIN REVOLUTION

Fulfillment or Betrayal of Communism?

EDITED WITH AN INTRODUCTION BY

Robert V. Daniels

UNIVERSITY OF VERMONT

D. C. HEATH AND COMPANY · BOSTON

Englewood · Chicago · Dallas · San Francisco · Atlanta

Library of Congress Catalog Card Number 64–8153

COPYRIGHT © 1965 BY D. C. HEATH AND COMPANY

Printed July 1966

Table of Contents

v

III. THE SOCIAL COUNTERREVOLUTION

IV. EVALUATIONS AND EXPLANATIONS

Introduction

THE "Stalin Revolution" refers to those years in the history of Soviet Russia in the late 1920's and early 1930's when Joseph Stalin, with the iron hand of his newly established dictatorship, imposed upon the country the essential forms of economic, social, and cultural organization which have characterized Soviet Communism ever since. As much or more than the Revolution of 1917, the Stalin Revolution must be understood by anyone who approaches the study of the Soviet Union, no matter whether he is working in the framework of a special discipline of social science — political science, economics, or sociology — or whether he proceeds from the general historical standpoint. The present collection of readings is offered, to begin with, as an important case study of one of the most important human phenomena of modern times.

But there are problems in studying the Soviet Union in general and the Stalin Revolution in particular that draw the student quickly and deeply into exciting and controversial issues — into the realm of historical opinion and judgment. For this reason the Stalin Revolution is a good topic for learning how to cope with the eternal historical problems of interpretation, bias, and conflict.

It goes without saying that any inquiry relating to the revolutionary movement of Communism arouses powerful feelings. This is humanly inevitable in dealing with any of the truly dramatic events and conflicts in history. When the student approaches Soviet Russia and Communism he will in all likelihood find strong emotions not only in the material he reads, but in himself as he reads it. This is inescapable, yet it cannot go uncontrolled, for it is death to serious history if feeling gets the upper hand over explanation.

Historical explanation requires the investigator to look at human affairs in a certain way, and this is a way that is often lacking in discussions of Communism — even by experts. History is above all the recognition of change in human affairs — the realization that changing or unforeseen circumstances may put people, their ideas, their actions in a very different context and alter the significance of all that is said or done. History can show how the unfolding future confounds human plans and intentions. History can make the present more realistically intelligible by showing how things really happen.

It would be absurd, in the light of this, to let the history of Soviet Russia rest with the simple triumph of the Communist revolution, whether viewed as good or evil. Citizens of Soviet Russia have had, since around 1929, little opportunity to discuss the meaning of changes in their own revolution, but outsiders in the West have less excuse for ignoring the vast historical developments which have gone on within the Soviet system, and the potential for further change as well. For the historian, the challenge is not just to relate himself to a movement, pro or con, but to penetrate the history of that movement and learn where, why, and how historical changes, for better or worse, have been going on in the movement itself.

There is no lack of historical study of the Soviet Union by serious scholars in the West, whether they are specialists in one of the areas of the social sciences, or historians concerning themselves with the total flow of events in time. From their work, together with the unofficial and official documentary source material which has emanated from the Soviet Union, the student can derive an immensely detailed and fairly reliable picture of Soviet history and Soviet life year by year. What is not immediately clear, however, is the explanation, the cause, the ultimate implication, of the events and changes which students of history observe.

All schools of thought about Soviet history acknowledge the years from 1929 to 1932 as a revolutionary turning point in the development of the Communist system, though they may differ widely in their estimates of the reasons, achievements, and implications of the changes which came about during this period. Stalin's policies — particularly the forced industrialization in the first Five-Year Plan, the elimination of all business and labor freedom, the collectivization of the peasants, the intensification of Communist party discipline and police measures, the imposition of totalitarian controls on cultural life, and the abandonment of libertarian social experiments — established the basic and enduring features of the Soviet regime which still exist.

The great question about the Stalin Revolution is its relation to the Communist revolution of 1917. Was the Stalin Revolution a direct continuation of Lenin's movement, the logical next step? Or was it a break away from the course of 1917, a new historical turning point, a betrayal of the hopes of the original revolution? The answer to these questions can have fundamental importance in understanding the nature of Soviet Russia and of the worldwide Communist movement. Has Communism evolved according to plan, in line with the original revolutionary impetus of its founders, or has it in some respects turned onto a new path where practice contradicts theory and where a native dictatorship contradicts the international mission?

The official Communist view of the Stalin Revolution, ever since the event, has presented it as the strict application of Marxist principles. Many Western writers agree, though in the eyes of some it only went from bad to worse. Dissident Marxists like Trotsky have held that Stalin's revolution was a profound betrayal of Communist principles. Other observers have taken the position that Russian circumstances, for better or worse, compelled Stalin to make fundamental changes in the Communist program. No one denies that crucial changes occurred in the Stalin Revolution, but why they occurred, and what they meant for the country's history, are questions that open the door to the most diverse interpretation. Was the Stalin Revolution a fulfillment — good or bad — of the Bolshevik promise of 1917? Or was it a betrayal — cynical or practical — of the aspirations of the October Revolution?

The actual steps of the Stalin Revolution were scarcely anticipated beforehand. The initial revolutionary period of terror, civil strife, and utopian experiment — the so-called era of "War Communism" — had been terminated by Lenin's adoption of the more moderate "New Economic Policy" or "NEP" in 1921. This permitted a money economy, salary differentials, individual farming, private ownership of small business (by the so-called "Nepmen"), and considerable intellectual freedom, all on the premise that the Marxist movement would have to mark time in Russia while it waited for world revolution to come to pass. The Communist Party — ruling as a one-party dictatorship but still enjoying some freedom of controversy within its ranks — fell to disputing over all manner of policy matters, and especially over the question of Russia's future industrial development.

The stakes were raised with Lenin's death in 1924 and the question of who would succeed to his post of leadership. Leon Trotsky, Gregory Zinoviev, and

Nikolai Bukharin bid one after another for the leadership of the party and government. Each in turn was defeated by the man who, as General Secretary since 1922, controlled the keys to power in the Communist Party organization — Joseph Stalin. Trotsky and Zinoviev, after belatedly combining forces, were crushed by Stalin and Bukharin in the party organizations in 1926 and 1927, and at the Fifteenth Party Congress in December 1927, the Trotskyists and Zinovievists were expelled from the Communist Party. Trotsky was exiled to Central Asia in January 1928, and in February 1929 he was deported from the USSR altogether. Meanwhile Stalin turned against the Right Opposition led by Bukharin (the party theoretician), Alexei Rykov (Lenin's successor as Prime Minister), and Mikhail Tomsky (the chief of the trade unions). Stalin easily defeated the Right Opposition in the fall of 1928, partly by borrowing arguments from the Trotskyists, and by the spring of 1929 he was to all intents and purposes an absolute personal dictator (even though he actually held no government post).

The rise of Stalin is recounted with great insight by Isaac Deutscher in his *Stalin: A Political Biography*, from which the first selection in this book is taken. Deutscher combines a Marxist recognition of the underlying social and economic forces with a stress on the personal impact of Stalin. He raises basic questions concerning both the source and the use of Stalin's power. The student should try to see how Stalin derived his power from the Communist Party organization, and then consider the question: Did this all-powerful dictator really abide by the perspective of Marxian socialism, or did he fundamentally alter the planned course of events in Russia?

Stalin's radical political and economic steps of 1929 were closely connected with the frustrating problems of economic backwardness and industrial development which Russia faced in the 1920's. Bitter controversies had been going on among the Communist leaders ever since 1921

over continuing the capitalistic concessions of the New Economic Policy or launching an ambitious governmental program of planned industrialization. These two alternatives — the "Right" policy of Bukharin and the "Left" program of Trotsky and Preobrazhensky — are discussed in the second selection in this book, from *The Soviet Industrialization Debate, 1924–1928*, by Alexander Erlich. Erlich suggests that the difficulties inherent in both the "Left" and "Right" proposals cast considerable doubt on the validity of the Marxian perspective for Russia. Did Stalin's ultimate answer — a violent break in agricultural and industrial policy — mean that Marxism was salvaged after all? Or is it more realistic to view it as a unique new program dictated by the problems of Russian backwardness?

Another problem is the manner in which Stalin arrived at the policies of the Stalin Revolution. Was he truly the far-sighted statesman pursuing a long-range plan? Or did day-to-day political questions contribute to his policy decisions? This question of how Stalin arrived at the decisions of the Stalin Revolution arises in the selection from my own book, *The Conscience of The Revolution: Communist Opposition in Soviet Russia*, where I describe Stalin's struggle with the Right Opposition led by Bukharin. There is reason to question whether policy differences were Stalin's reason for fighting the Bukharin group, or whether the issues were contrived as weapons of political warfare against his rivals in a power struggle.

Following his victory over the Right Opposition, Stalin intensified his dictatorial control over the country through the agencies of the secret police and the Communist Party organization. He made special efforts to impose controls on intellectual life — the writers, artists, scientists, and even Communist theorists. He brought about a substantial change in the official Soviet interpretation of Marxism, which is described in the selection taken from the theoretical introduction to Raymond Bauer's *New Man in Soviet Psychology*. The question raised here is fundamental in understanding the relation between Marxist theory and Soviet policy: Were Stalin and his followers making a genuine effort to clarify the "activist" truth of Marxism, or were they trying to get around the theory where it appeared to balk their determination to overhaul the Russian economy by political command? Was the Stalin Revolution based on a real revival of Marxism or a cynical manipulation of it?

The two greatest policy innovations of the Stalin Revolution were the collectivization of the peasants and the Five-Year Plan of intensive industrialization. Actually, neither of these programs was original with Stalin — he borrowed them mainly from the Trotskyists, in an exaggerated form, with the immediate political purpose of discrediting the Bukharinists. By the end of 1929 industrialization and collectivization were in full swing, and in his public speeches Stalin was congratulating himself already on the victory of Marxism over Russian backwardness. These claims are illustrated by the two selections from the speeches in Stalin's *Problems of Leninism*. According to Stalin there was only one alternative — his own — apart from surrender to the forces of capitalism. But as the judgments of such economists as Alec Nove suggest, there is reason to doubt that Stalin's high-speed program was really the most effective path to industrialization.

Nove, in his article, "Was Stalin Really Necessary?" undertakes to show the assumptions and decisions that made Stalin's revolution, his economic and political harshness, and at least some of his cruelties, more or less unavoidable. He raises the question whether any determined group of rulers in Russia's economic circumstances could maintain their domestic and international power without resort to some of the methods of Stalinism.

In the course of Stalin's industrial drive, many of the Marxist ideas and practices previously upheld by the Soviet authorities were sacrificed in the name of industrial efficiency. This was especially striking in the case of industrial labor, where revolutionary hopes for equality and industrial self-government gave way to bureaucratic power, inequality, and impoverishment of the workers. Part of Stalin's struggle with the Right Opposition involved a fight to remove Bukharin's ally Mikhail Tomsky from the trade union leadership because he wanted the unions to represent the workers in any conflict with the state. This is recounted in the selection from Manya Gordon's history of Russian labor, *Workers Before and After Lenin*. She raises the question of what, after all, the "dictatorship of the proletariat" was supposed to mean for the proletariat itself. Stalin's policies as she describes them meant a dismal deterioration in the proletariat's conditions of working and living. Was this necessary to Stalin's industrial plans, and if so, what was the real objective of the plans?

The collectivization of Soviet agriculture which paralleled the First Five-Year Plan was carried out with even less regard for the rights and interests of the people concerned. This is made undeniably clear in the selection from Merle Fainsod's *Soviet Rule in Smolensk*, a remarkable book based on captured Soviet documents. Fainsod's material suggests that such ruthlessness was inherent in the Communist Party dictatorship, though it could perhaps be argued that the brutalizing conditions of Russian rural backwardness and old class feuds among the peasants were responsible for carrying local atrocities beyond anything the leadership intended.

What might be termed the secondary effects of Stalin's industrialization and collectivization drive were responses to the problems which the drive revealed or to the opposition which it engendered. It was in these years that Soviet society became fully totalitarian, in the sense of tight party control not only in political affairs but over all aspects of life. Autonomous economic activity came to an end with the nationalization of the small businesses of the "Nepmen"; the subordination of the trade unions to the interests of production; and the elimination of individual farming. The basic social policies of the government — up to then a mixture of utopianism tempered by expediency — were deliberately revised in the direction of conservatism and discipline. In the official view, these changes were intended to eliminate "petty-bourgeois" notions of equality and individual freedom. The sociological appraisal by Barrington Moore, contained in the selection from *Soviet Politics: The Dilemma of Power,* suggests a contrary appraisal: to what extent did Stalin's acceptance of bureaucratic organization and inequality represent a permanent adjustment away from the Revolution and toward conservatism?

Similar shifts of policy can be discerned in other fields — in Soviet education, for example, as George S. Counts maintains in the selection from *The Challenge of Soviet Education.* Counts describes the atmosphere of "progressive" educational experimentation in Russia in the 1920's, and the abrupt rejection of such experiments when Stalin's industrialization program put a premium on mass training and sheer literacy. Again, the question is whether Stalin was finally getting Soviet Russia on the correct Marxist track, or whether the requirements of political survival in industrial society compelled him to abandon the revolutionary ideal.

Most fields of intellectual life felt the heavy hand of tightened Communist Party control during the Stalin Revolution. Party dictation was particularly severe in the field of literature, as is depicted in the passages from *The Proletarian Episode in Russian Literature* by the American literary historian Edward Brown. The controls on literature, like other aspects of Stalin's policy, raise the question whether Stalin's intensification of the Communist dictatorship was not so great in degree as to make it different in kind as well. A particular issue in the case of literature is whether the ruling Averbakh group of the First Five-Year Plan period were purged because they resisted Stalin's crude Marx-

ist demands, or because they themselves were too doctrinaire to adjust their notions of "proletarian literature" to the propaganda requirements of the Stalin Revolution.

The harshness of Stalin's policies was not accepted by his subordinates without dissent. Although Bukharin's Right Opposition had been defeated by 1929, similar objections to Stalin's violent methods were widespread within the Communist Party, and Bukharin and his friends remained at liberty with minor government jobs. The hopes of the anti-Stalinists rested with the Leningrad party secretary, Sergei Kirov, who appeared to have some success in 1933 and 1934 in promoting a relaxation in some of Stalin's policies. Stalin, however, was preparing to destroy all who stood in his way. He was probably responsible for the assassination of Kirov in December 1934. The Great Purge of 1936–1938 soon followed. In 1936, when his own days were numbered, Bukharin gave the outside world an account of the intrigues in the Soviet leadership and the old Communist's sense of betrayal at Stalin's hands. Excerpts appear here from the edition published anonymously in New York, the *Letter of an Old Bolshevik.* They reveal to the reader the sense of total disillusionment — whether tragic awakening or sour grapes — felt by a Communist has-been, as he viewed the aftermath of the Stalin Revolution.

The final section of this book contains five selections representing a variety of overall evaluations of the years of the Stalin Revolution in Soviet Russia. Walter Duranty, in the despatches he wrote from Paris in 1931, took the historical approach — Stalin was to him a very Russian and even Asiatic phenomenon, though the student may find this point of view too simplistic and even mystical. Rudolf Schlesinger, in *The Spirit of Post-War Russia,* combined a similar recognition of the Russian environment with a Marxist view of the requirements of the Revolution, and this led to an apology for Stalin far franker than Stalin himself would admit.

Thanks to the control which the party exercised over all media of communication, it was possible for Stalin to describe every aspect of his revolution as the necessary and proper development of Marxism-Leninism and the dictatorship of the proletariat. This position is still held by the official Communist historians, including Boris Ponomarev, the chief editor of the most recent official *History of the Communist Party of the Soviet Union.* As the selection from this volume shows, Stalin's personal role has been minimized, but the Communist Party gets credit for faithfully implementing the Marxist ideal of socialist industry and collective agriculture. Bearing in mind that this is an official text for an audience that cannot compare it with other sources, the reader might ask himself what distortions had to be introduced to sustain the picture of Soviet history presently demanded by the party authorities. Does it suggest that Stalin has really been repudiated?

Here, as everywhere in the study of Soviet affairs, the student should be cautioned not to accept uncritically the theoretical claims of the Soviet leadership and assume that the theory of Marxism really has guided and explained the development of Soviet society. Rudolph Hilferding, an eminent theorist of democratic Marxism, faced this problem squarely in his famous article, "State Capitalism or Totalitarian State Economy" (included here in full). Hilferding goes so far in revising the Marxist estimate of Soviet Russia that he may seem to have abandoned the Marxist framework of explanation altogether.

The final selection from Trotsky's *Revolution Betrayed* is a moral protest from the defeated candidate for dictator. Trotsky raises all of the great problems of interpreting the Stalin Revolution: Was it as bad as he says? Was it the personal work of one man, suggesting that a Trotsky Revolution would have been better? Or was it the only way to rule successfully, given Russia's internal and international circumstances? And if it was dictated by circumstances, were these the circumstances foreseen by Marxism such as would make for the dictatorship of the proletariat, or were they circumstances of another sort facilitating the dictatorship of somebody else?

An overall review of the materials on the Stalin Revolution cannot fail to bring some profound problems into focus. The Stalin Revolution was an unprecedented event, calling for some particular explanation in terms of the individual, the political institutions, the economic circumstances, and the national experience. As an aspect of the history of Communism, the Stalin Revolution requires some appraisal of the truth and relevance of Marxist theory, and of the relation between theory and actual Communist behavior. Finally, outside the Communist frame of reference altogether, the reader may wish to make his own informed moral judgments about the good or evil of the Stalin Revolution, or about its necessity and its achievements. Was the Stalin Revolution in some way justified, whether from the standpoint of theoretical ideals, national power, or everyday progress, or was it an unredeemed historic crime?

The Conflict of Opinion

"The root difference between Stalinism and the traditional Socialist outlook lay in their respective attitudes towards the role of force in the transformation of society."

— ISAAC DEUTSCHER

"Stalin . . . was determined to maneuver those who held to the old official policy into a position where they appeared to be deviators."

— ROBERT V. DANIELS

"By force of circumstances, the least theoretically minded of Bolshevik leaders seems to have become the sponsor of one of the most sophisticated and possibly the most sophistic of theories."

— RAYMOND A. BAUER

"Trotskyism's Menshevik 'conception' that the working class is incapable of leading the great bulk of the peasantry in the cause of Socialist construction is collapsing and being smashed to atoms."

— JOSEPH V. STALIN

"Stalin's attitude towards labor was precisely the same as that of the early Russian capitalists towards the erstwhile serfs."

— MANYA GORDON

"The whole-hog Stalin . . . was not necessary but the possibility of a Stalin was a necessary consequence of the effort of a minority group to keep power and to carry out a vast social-economic revolution in a very short time."

— ALEC NOVE

"Stalin emphasized what Lenin had merely suggested — that inequality served a necessary social function in a socialist as well as in a capitalist society. It is this point which constitutes a new element in Russian Marxist ideology."

— BARRINGTON MOORE

"The Soviet leaders . . . became painfully aware of the general backwardness of Russia. . . . As a consequence, a new Soviet school emerged . . . which resembled in many respects the school of old Russia and would have been labeled counterrevolutionary in the earlier period, but one which in fact expresses the basic philosophy of Bolshevism far more faithfully than its predecessor."

— George S. Counts

"Stalin reasoned . . . : If the old Bolsheviks, the group constituting today the ruling caste in the country, are unfit to perform this function, it is necessary to remove them from their posts, to create *a new ruling caste.*"

— Nikolai Bukharin

"To the Russian people the Five-Year Plan . . . is a goal to aim at, and its inception cannot but be regarded as a stroke of genius by anyone familiar with the Russian nature."

— Walter Duranty

"The foundations of Socialism had been laid in the Soviet Union. . . . The question: 'Who will beat whom?,' posed by Lenin, had been settled in favor of Socialism. . . . This was an *epoch-making* victory of the working class, working peasantry and intelligentsia of the USSR, won under the leadership of the Communist Party."

— Boris N. Ponomaryov et al.

"History, this 'best of all Marxists,' has taught us differently. It has taught us that 'administering of things,' despite Engels' expectations, may turn into unlimited 'administering of people,' and thus not only lead to the emancipation of the state from the economy but even to the subjection of the economy to the state."

— Rudolf Hilferding

"The Stalin regime, rising above a politically atomized society, resting upon a police and officers' corps, and allowing of no control whatever, is obviously a variation of Bonapartism. . . ."

— Leon Trotsky

I. THE SETTING

The Leader and the Party

ISAAC DEUTSCHER

The lever for setting the Stalin Revolution in motion was the personal dictatorship which Joseph Stalin had established over the Russian Communist Party. One of the best-known accounts of Stalin's rise to power is the work of Isaac Deutscher (1907–   ), a native of Poland and a one-time Communist and Trotskyist, who now lives in England and devotes himself to historical and political writing on the Soviet Union. Deutscher tries to show how Stalin combined organizational loyalty and shrewd maneuver to clear the path for his own supreme power.

Few important developments in history are so inconspicuous and seem so inconsequential to their contemporaries as did the amazing accumulation of power in the hands of Stalin, which took place while Lenin was still alive. Two years after the end of the civil war Russian society already lived under Stalin's virtual rule, without being aware of the ruler's name. More strangely still, he was voted and moved into all his positions of power by his rivals. There was to be an abundance of sombre drama in his later fight against these rivals. But the fight began only after he had firmly gripped all the levers of power and after his opponents, awakening to his role, had tried to move him from his dominant position. But then they found him immovable. . . .

. . . The day-to-day management of the party belonged to Stalin. The Politbureau discussed high policy. Another body, which was, like the Politbureau, elected by the Central Committee, the Organization Bureau (Orgbureau), was in charge of the party's personnel, which it was free to call up, direct to work, and distribute throughout the army and the civil service according to the demands of the civil war. From the beginning of 1919 Stalin was the only permanent liaison officer between the Politbureau and the Orgbureau. He ensured the unity of policy and organization; that is, he marshalled the forces of the party according to the Politbureau's directives. Like none of his colleagues, he was immersed in the party's daily drudgery and in all its kitchen cabals.

At this stage his power was already formidable. Still more was to accrue to him from his appointment, on 3 April 1922, to the post of General Secretary of the Central Committee. The eleventh congress of the party had just elected a new and enlarged Central Committee and again modified the statutes. The leading bodies of the party were now top-heavy; and a new office, that of the General Secretary, was created, which was to co-ordinate the work of their many growing and overlapping branches. It was on that occasion, Trotsky alleges, that Lenin aired, in the

From *Stalin: A Political Biography* by Isaac Deutscher. Copyright 1949 by Oxford University Press. Pp. 228, 231–233, 235–236, 256–257, 273–275, 294–296, 314–317, 343–344. Reprinted by permission.

1

inner circle of his associates, his misgivings about Stalin's candidature: "This cook can only serve peppery dishes." But his doubts were, at any rate, not grave; and he himself in the end sponsored the candidature of the "cook." Molotov and Kuibychev were appointed Stalin's assistants, the former having already been one of the secretaries of the party. The appointment was reported in the Russian press without any ado, as a minor event in the inner life of the party.

Soon afterwards a latent dualism of authority began to develop at the very top of the party. The seven men who now formed the Politbureau (in addition to the previous five,[1] Zinoviev and Tomsky had recently been elected) represented, as it were, the brain and the spirit of Bolshevism. In the offices of the General Secretariat resided the more material power of management and direction. In name the General Secretariat was subordinate to the illustrious and exalted Politbureau. But the dependence of the Politbureau on the Secretariat became so great that without that prop the Politbureau looked more and more like a body awkwardly suspended in a void. The Secretariat prepared the agenda for each session of the Politbureau. It supplied the documentation on every point under debate. It transmitted the Politbureau's decisions to the lower grades. It was in daily contact with the many thousands of party functionaries in the capital and the provinces. It was responsible for their appointments, promotions, and demotions. It could, up to a point, prejudice the views of the Politbureau on any issue before it came up for debate. It could twist the practical execution of the Politbureau's decisions, according to the tastes of the General Secretary. Similar bodies exist in any governmental machinery but rarely acquire independent authority. What usually prevents them from transgressing their terms of reference is some diffusion of power through the whole system of government, effective control over them, and, sometimes, the integrity of officials. The over-centralization of power in the Bolshevik leadership, the lack of effective control, and, last but not least, the personal ambitions of the General Secretary, all made for the extraordinary weight that the General Secretariat began to carry barely a few months after it had been set up. . . .

Stalin was in a sense less dependent on Lenin than were his colleagues; his intellectual needs were more limited than theirs. He was interested in the practical use of the Leninist gadgets, not in the Leninist laboratory of thought. His own behavior was now dictated by the moods, needs, and pressures of the vast political machine that he had come to control. His political philosophy boiled down to securing the dominance of that machine by the handiest and most convenient means. In an avowedly dictatorial régime, repression often is the handiest and most convenient method of action. The Politbureau may have been thrown into disarray by Lenin's disappearance; the General Secretariat was not. On the contrary, since it had no longer to account for what it did to the vigilant and astute supervisor, it acted with greater firmness and self-confidence. . . . The General Secretary knew how to justify each act of repression against malcontent Bolsheviks in the light of the party statutes as they had, on Lenin's initiative and with Trotsky's support, been amended by the tenth and eleventh congresses. He was careful to explain every step he made as an inevitable consequence of decisions previously adopted by common consent. He packed the offices with his friends, henchmen, and followers, the men of Baku and Tsaritsyn.[2] Dismissed malcontents complained to the Politbureau, where Trotsky took up their cases. In reply, Stalin referred to the commonly agreed

[1] Lenin, Trotsky, Stalin, Kamenev, and Rykov. [Editor's note.]

[2] A reference to the pre-revolutionary Bolshevik organization in the city of Baku, and to the fighting at Tsaritsyn (later Stalingrad, now Volgograd) during the Russian Civil War. [Editor's note.]

division of responsibilities: the Politbureau was to pass decisions on matters of high policy; the General Secretariat and the Orgbureau were in charge of the party's personnel. The Politbureau was only bored with Trotsky's carping criticisms. . . .

To be able to marshal its forces, the personnel department kept solid files with the most detailed records of the party's "key-men." The party had now, after the first purges, about 400,000 ordinary members and about 20,000 officials. So far the personnel department had compiled the records of the upper and medium layers, including 1,300 managers of industry. The investigation, Stalin disclosed, was still on. The files were compiled with special attention to every member's professional skill and specialization, political reliability, and moral bearings. Every blemish in a member's record was duly registered. "It is necessary to study every worker through and through," said Stalin, "in every detail." "Otherwise policy loses sense and becomes meaningless gesticulation." Since the personnel department had to meet or help in meeting any demand for officials, it had spread a network of branches throughout the country. It had the power to order members to change their occupation and place of residence at the shortest notice, to shift from the capital to the wilderness of Siberia or to an embassy abroad, in order to carry out any assignment. An assignment, even an honourable one, might be a pretext for the punishment of a somewhat restive member. Few persons, whatever their merits, could have been quite sure that if their politics displeased the General Secretariat, some *faux pas* committed by them in the past would not now be publicly held out against them. But, so far, this had not become common practice.

The General Secretary was also responsible for appointments of provincial party leaders. He spoke about this with specious sadness. It was time, he told the congress,

that provincial organizations elected their secretaries, instead of getting them appointed from above. Unfortunately, the lack of qualified men was so acute that local branches were all the time pestering the General Secretariat to send them people from the centre. "It is very difficult to train party leaders. This requires five, ten, or even more years. It is much easier to conquer this or that country with the help of Comrade Budienny's cavalry than to train two or three leaders from the rank and file." He defended the provincial committees that had so often been attacked and ridiculed in the newspapers. He spoke for the whole phalanx of his secretaries; and he excused even their squabbling and intriguing, which had their good as well as their bad sides, because they helped in the crystallization of "coherent nuclei of leaders." In other words, the provincial committees were miniature replicas of the Politbureau with their own little triumvirates and duumvirates and their groups of oppositionists. . . .

. . . It had always been admitted that history might repeat itself; and that a Directory[3] or a single usurper might once again climb to power on the back of the revolution. It was taken for granted that the Russian usurper would, like his French prototype, be a personality possessed of brilliance and legendary fame won in battles. The mask of Bonaparte seemed to fit Trotsky only too well. Indeed, it might have fitted any personality with the exception of Stalin. In this lay part of his strength.

The very thing which under different circumstances would have been a liability in a man aspiring to power, his obscurity, was his important asset. The party had been brought up to distrust "bourgeois individualism" and to strive for collectivism. None of its leaders looked as immune

[3] Refers to the Directory in Revolutionary France from 1795 to 1799, a regime which represented a step backward for the revolution. [Editor's note.]

from the former and as expressive of the
latter as Stalin. What was striking in the
General Secretary was that there was
nothing striking about him. His almost
impersonal personality seemed to be the
ideal vehicle for the anonymous forces of
class and party. His bearing seemed of the
utmost modesty. He was more accessible
to the average official or party man than
the other leaders. He studiously cultivated
his contacts with the people who in one
way or another made and unmade reputa-
tions, provincial secretaries, popular satiri-
cal writers, and foreign visitors. Himself
taciturn, he was unsurpassed at the art of
patiently listening to others. Sometimes
he would be seen in a corner of a staircase
pulling at his pipe and listening immov-
ably, for an hour or two, to an agitated
interlocutor and breaking his silence only
to ask a few questions. This was one of his
qualities that seemed to indicate a lack of
any egotism. The interviewer, glad of the
opportunity to get his troubles off his chest,
rarely reflected on the fact that Stalin
had not revealed his mind in the conversation. For Stalin, to quote his secretary,
"did not confide his innermost thoughts to
anybody. Only very rarely did he share his
ideas and impressions with his closest associates. He possessed in a high degree
the gift for silence, and in this respect he
was unique in a country where everybody
talked far too much."

His private life, too, was beyond re-
proach or suspicion. "This passionate politician [says Bazhanov] has no other vices.
He loves neither money, nor pleasure,
neither sport, nor women. Women, apart
from his own wife, do not exist for him."
In the middle of the civil war he married
for the second time. His wife, Nadezhda
Alliluyeva, the daughter of the workman in
whose home Lenin hid in the July days
of 1917, was twenty years younger than
himself. She had been one of Lenin's secretaries after the revolution and went to
Tsaritsyn in 1919. There the love between
the Commissar and the Communist girl
began. Now they had a small lodging in

what used to be the servants' quarters in
the Kremlin; and Nadezhda Alliluyeva
was earnestly studying at a technical college in Moscow. The air of plainness and
even austerity about the General Secretary's private life commended him to the
puritanically minded party, which was just
beginning to grow apprehensive at the first
signs of corruption and loose life in the
Kremlin.

Nor did Stalin at that time impress people as being more intolerant than befitted
a Bolshevik leader. He was, as we have
seen, less vicious in his attacks on the opposition than the other triumvirs. In his
speeches there was usually the tone of a
good-natured and soothing, if facile, optimism, which harmonized well with the
party's growing complacency. In the Politbureau, when matters of high policy were
under debate, he never seemed to impose
his views on his colleagues. He carefully
followed the course of the debate to see
which way the wind was blowing and invariably voted with the majority, unless
he had assured his majority beforehand.
He was therefore always agreeable to the
majority. To party audiences he appeared
as a man without personal grudge and ran-
cour, as a detached Leninist, a guardian
of the doctrine who criticized others only
for the sake of the cause. . . .

In 1929, five years after Lenin's death,
Soviet Russia embarked upon her second
revolution, which was directed solely and
exclusively by Stalin. In its scope and immediate impact upon the life of some 160
million people the second revolution was
even more sweeping and radical than the
first. It resulted in Russia's rapid industrialization; it compelled more than a hundred million peasants to abandon their
small, primitive holdings and to set up collective farms; it ruthlessly tore the pri-
meval wooden plough from the hands of
the *muzhik* [peasant] and forced him to
grasp the wheel of a modern tractor; it
drove tens of millions of illiterate people

to school and made them learn to read and write; and spiritually it detached European Russia from Europe and brought Asiatic Russia nearer to Europe. The rewards of that revolution were astounding; but so was its cost: the complete loss, by a whole generation, of spiritual and political freedom. It takes a great effort of the imagination to gauge the enormousness and the complexity of that upheaval for which hardly any historical precedent can be found. Even if all allowance is made for the different scales of human affairs in different ages, the greatest reformers in Russian history, Ivan the Terrible and Peter the Great, and the great reformers of other nations too, seem to be drawfed by the giant form of the General Secretary.

And yet the giant's robe hangs somewhat loosely upon Stalin's figure. There is a baffling disproportion between the magnitude of the second revolution and the stature of its maker, a disproportion which was not noticeable in the revolution of 1917. There the leaders seem to be equal to the great events; here the events seem to reflect their greatness upon the leader. Lenin and Trotsky foresaw their revolution and prepared it many years before it materialized. Their own ideas fertilized the soil of Russia for the harvest of 1917. Not so with Stalin. The ideas of the second revolution were not his. He neither foresaw it nor prepared for it. Yet he, and in a sense he alone, accomplished it. He was at first almost whipped into the vast undertaking by immediate dangers. He started it gropingly, and despite his own fears. Then, carried on by the force of his own doings, he walked the giant's causeway, almost without halt or rest. Behind him were tramping the myriads of weary and bleeding Russian feet, a whole generation in search of socialism in one country. His figure seemed to grow to mythical dimensions. Seen at close quarters, it was still the figure of a man of very ordinary stature and of middling thoughts. Only his fists and feet contrasted with his real stature—they were the fists and the feet of a giant.

. . . Since then Stalin's Communist opponents have repeatedly described him as the leader of an anti-revolutionary reaction, while most anti-Communists have seen and still see the haunting spectre of communism embodied in his person. Yet, among the Bolshevik leaders of the twenties, he was primarily the man of the golden mean. He instinctively abhorred the extreme viewpoints which then competed for the party's recognition. His peculiar job was to produce the formulas in which the opposed extremes seemed reconciled. To the mass of hesitating members of the party his words sounded like common sense itself. They accepted his leadership in the hope that the party would be reliably steered along the "middle of the road" and that "safety first" would be the guiding principle. It might be said that he appeared as the Baldwin or the Chamberlain,[4] the Harding or the Hoover of Bolshevism, if the mere association of those names with Bolshevism did not sound too incongruous.

It was neither Stalin's fault nor his merit that he never succeeded in sticking to the middle of any road; and that he was constantly compelled to abandon "safety" for the most dangerous of ventures. Revolutions are as a rule intolerant of golden means and "common sense." Those who in a revolution try to tread the middle of the road usually find the earth cleaving under their feet. Stalin was repeatedly compelled to make sudden and inordinately violent jumps now to this now to that extreme of the road. . . .

. . . The defeat of each successive opposition violently narrowed the margins within which the free expression of opinion was possible. The leaders of each opposition could not get for themselves more elbow room than that to which they themselves, in coalition with Stalin, had reduced their adversaries. After each

[4] References to the British Conservative prime ministers of the 1920's and '30's. [Editor's note.]

showdown, actions hitherto regarded as unimpeachable were classed as unpardonable. . . . Only specific offences against discipline, clandestine printings, and unauthorized street demonstrations, offences into which Stalin had provoked his adversaries, could justify reprisals against the opposition in 1927. Less than a year later a whispered conversation between a member of the Politbureau and a repentant leader of the opposition, the conversation between Bukharin and Kamenev, was already a grave offence, for which Bukharin tearfully begged pardon from the Politbureau. The alternative to submission was an ostracism doubly unbearable; for it was pronounced against the "offender" not by a class enemy but by his associate in the revolution, and it left the "offender" incapable even of crying in the wilderness. . . .

After Stalin had finally removed Trotsky from the Russian scene, he hastened to rout the leaders of the right wing. Rykov was deposed from the Premiership of the Soviet Government, in which he had succeeded Lenin. Tomsky was ousted from the leadership of the trade unions, on the ground that he had used his influence to turn the unions against industrialization. Bukharin was dismissed from the leadership of the Communist International, where he had replaced Zinoviev, as well as from the Politbureau. Before the year 1929 was out, Bukharin, Rykov, and Tomsky repudiated their own views and thus bought a few years of spurious breathing space.

Stalin's ascendancy was now complete. The contest for power was at its end. All his rivals had been eliminated. None of the members of the Politbureau would dream of challenging his authority. In the last days of the year Moscow celebrated his fiftieth birthday as if it had been a great historic event. From every corner of Russia tributes were addressed to the Leader. His virtues were praised, immoderately and crudely, by every party secretary in the country. The walls of Moscow were covered with his huge portraits. His statues and busts of all possible sizes filled the squares, the halls of public buildings, and the windows of every shop down to the humblest barber's shop. "Stalin is the Lenin of to-day," the propagandists shouted themselves hoarse. Some of the older people recalled Lenin's fiftieth birthday. It had been a small and modest occasion, which Lenin reluctantly attended only to remonstrate with his admirers for their growing fondness for pomp and ceremony. The new Stalinist cult was now visibly merging with the old Leninist cult, and overshadowing it. When, on ceremonial occasions, Stalin appeared at the top of the Lenin mausoleum in the Red Square, Lenin's colossal tomb appeared to be only the pedestal for his successor. . . .

It is easy to see how far Stalin drifted away from what had hitherto been the main stream of Socialist and Marxist thought. What his socialism had in common with the new society, as it had been imagined by Socialists of nearly all shades, was public ownership of the means of production and planning. It differed in the degradation to which it subjected some sections of the community and also in the recrudescence of glaring social inequalities amid the poverty which the revolution inherited from the past. But the root difference between Stalinism and the traditional Socialist outlook lay in their respective attitudes towards the role of force in the transformation of society.

Marxism was, as it were, the illegitimate and rebellious offspring of nineteenth-century liberalism. Bitterly opposed to its parent, it had many a feature in common with it. The prophets of *laisser faire* had deprecated political force, holding that it could play no progressive role in social life. In opposition to liberalism, Marxists stressed those historic instances and situations in which — as in the English and French revolutions, the American War of Independence and the Civil War — force did assist in the progress of nations and classes. But they also held that the limits within which political force could effect changes in the outlook of society were narrow. They held that the fortunes of peoples were shaped primarily by basic economic and social processes; and that, compared with these, force could play only a subordinate role. Much as the Marxist and the Liberal ideals of society differed from one another, both trends shared, in different degrees, the optimism about the future of modern civilization, so characteristic of the nineteenth century. Each of the two trends assumed that the progress of modern society tended more or less spontaneously towards the attainment of its ideal. Marx and Engels expressed their common view in the famous phrase that force is the midwife of every old society pregnant with a new one. The midwife merely helps the baby to leave the mother's womb when the time for that has come. She can do no more. Stalin's view on the role of political force, reflected in his deeds rather than his words, oozes the atmosphere of twentieth-century totalitarianism. Stalin might have paraphrased the old Marxian aphorism: force is no longer the midwife — force is the mother of the new society.

The Problem of Industrial Development

ALEXANDER ERLICH

Alexander Erlich (1912–   ) is Professor of Economics at Columbia University and a specialist on the history of Soviet economic doctrines. Polish born, he was the son of Henryk Erlich, a noted leader of the Jewish Socialist Bund, executed by the Russians in 1941. Professor Erlich nevertheless writes with remarkable objectivity about the efforts of various Communist schools of thought—Left, Right, and Stalinist Center—to find a successful path to socialism which would surmount the difficulties of the backward Russian environment. He finds in the end that economic realities made the best ideals of the revolution a tragic impossibility.

THE years 1924–1928 witnessed a remarkable debate in the Soviet Union. Its major participants were leading Communist theoreticians and eminent nonparty economists; the keenly interested audience included everyone who was politically and intellectually articulate in Soviet society. The debate ranged far and wide from issues concerning the theory of value to day-to-day political minutiae. At its center, overshadowing all the rest, loomed the problem of the appropriate speed and pattern for the prospective economic development of the country. . . .

. . . The successes of the NEP carried the Soviet economy beyond the range in which immediate survival was at stake, and enhanced the state's power to influence the course of events not merely by desisting from wrong-headed interference. But the jolts of imbalances and the steadily approaching ceilings for smooth increases

Reprinted by permission of the author and publishers from Alexander Erlich, *The Soviet Industrialization Debate, 1924–1928.* Cambridge, Mass.: Harvard University Press, 1950 (Russian Research Center Studies, no. 41); Copyright by the President and Fellows of Harvard College. Pp. xv, xvii, xx–xxi, 31–32, 34–35, 56–59, 79, 88–89, 164–165, 180–182.

indicated clearly that recovery was drawing to a close and that an enlargement of the capacity for growth was necessary. In Soviet parlance, the transition from "restoration" to "reconstruction" was impending. The perspective of protracted isolation within a hostile and much more powerful world, finally, made it imperative for the country to rely in this expansion upon its own resources, to a much greater extent than had been true of Tsarist Russia, or than had been hoped for in those heady years when the frontiers of the revolution seemed to lie on the Rhine. . . .

. . . The Soviet economic advance since 1928 has been one of the dominant facts of our time: there are few equally monumental truisms one can utter these days. The broad outlines of the pattern which emerged at the very beginning of the process have since then become familiar: a rate of investment set at a level which has few, if any, equals in the development of capitalist economies over a comparably long stretch of time; the overriding priority of producers' goods over consumers' goods in terms of the relative amount and quality of resources allotted to them; the change in terms of trade against agriculture, carried to unusual lengths for a country meeting the bulk of its food requirements from its own production. The results are history. According to the virtually unanimous view of Western students, the expansion of the Soviet industrial capacity has proceeded at a rate which is, by any meaningful standard of comparison, unprecedented. It is equally uncontroversial that this formidable drive, which has propelled the Soviet Union into the position of one of the two superpowers of the world, has entailed not only untold sacrifices in the welfare of the Soviet population but also grave risks for its rulers. Lags in low priority areas have resulted every now and then in major bottlenecks; convulsive shakeups and persistent all-pervading stresses and strains have cut into the efficiency of the huge investment efforts and have weakened the stability of

the economy. Indeed, there is every indication that the whole system was more than once on the verge of explosion during its initial years.

What were the alternatives open to the Soviet economy at the end of the twenties? To what degree were Soviet leaders aware of their nature and potentialities? Did the actual course of events follow a design laid down well in advance or was it, to a significant extent, an improvised response to circumstances? These questions are central to the understanding and appraisal of the Soviet experience in accelerated industrialization. . . .

. . . Evgeni A. Preobrazhenski, who had been Bukharin's comrade-in-arms in the latter's Left Communist period . . . , was . . . the chief economic theorist of the renascent left opposition, led by Trotsky. It was not surprising that the challenge to the "ideology of the restoration period" came from this side. The left-wing Communists wanted to solve the harrowing problems of a socialist regime in a backward Russia, faced with advanced capitalist countries, by aiming at a resumption of all-out revolutionary action in the West and at the rapid growth of the industrial proletariat at home. The less chance the first part of the blueprint had in the immediate future, the stronger was the emphasis put on the second. The time had come, it was felt, to turn the tables against the "private sector," first of all against the peasantry which had imposed upon the Soviet regime the retreat toward the "mixed economy" of the NEP and which was certain to bring about a full-scale restoration of capitalism unless drastically reduced in its social and economic weight. The task consisted in stating the case not in terms of wishful thinking or nostalgic longing for the "heroic period of the Russian revolution" but in the language of present-day realities and necessities. . . .

. . . [As Preobrazhenski saw it,] the

impact of revolutionary change had upset the precarious equilibrium of the Russian economy not only from the side of supply but also from that of demand. The share of industrial labor in national income had increased: "Our present wages are determined to a lesser extent than before the war by the value of labor power and in the future will be even less determined by it." Of still greater portent, however, was the transformation in the status of the peasantry. In Tsarist Russia a large portion of the income originating in peasant agriculture was absorbed by payments to the government and landlords. In order to get the money for the fulfillment of these obligations, the peasant had to sell a corresponding part of his produce without buying anything in return. This had a twofold effect. On the one hand, a relatively large marketable surplus of agricultural goods was provided; on the other, the claims of the great majority of the population upon industrial output were reduced by the sum total of these "forced sales." The amount deducted from peasant income was undoubtedly respent in the main. This reexpenditure, however, absorbed a smaller share of domestic output than a corresponding amount of peasant spending would have done; a large part of it (together with a sizeable fraction of industrial profits) went abroad either to service the foreign debt or as payment for imported luxury consumption goods, while its physical counterpart was exported. The October Revolution put an end to the old system. Rent payments were wiped out and agricultural taxes amounted in 1924–1925 to less than one-third of the total peasant obligations before the war. The unstabilizing effects of this upheaval were momentous:

Out of a given amount of the marketable output . . . a much smaller amount than before the war is going for forced sales; this means that the effective demand of the peasantry for industrial commodities and for the products of interpeasant exchange must correspondingly increase. . . . [Consequently] the stabilization of the relation between the total volume of the industrial and of the agricultural marketable output at the level of their prewar proportions implies a drastic disturbance in the equilibrium between the effective demand of the village and the marketable output of the town.

The conclusion was clear — productive capacity had to increase over and above the prewar level in order to catch up with the increased effective demand. The failure to accomplish this would result in a recurrence of the goods famine a few years hence, just as the failure to make sufficient provision for capital maintenance in the past made inevitable the present goods famine. . . .

. . . While the large addition to the existing stock of capital could be expected to have most salutary effects on the supply situation in the future, the investment which was necessary for producing this addition was bound to make things worse for the time being. Preobrazhenski, in fact, said this quite explicitly when he stated that "a discontinuous reconstruction of fixed capital involves a shift of so much means of production toward the production of means of production, which will yield output only after a few years, that thereby the increase of the consumption funds of the society will be stopped." He did not, however, add the inevitable conclusion that the amount of consumption goods per employed worker would decline.

In such a situation an uncontrolled economy could not avoid a wage-price spiral; but neither would the "workers' state" acting in accordance with Preobrazhenski's directives be able to keep the wages down in order to prevent an inflation. The shift of the main burden of the sacrifice to the nonindustrial population was the remaining alternative. This was what Preobrazhenski actually proposed to do by his policy of "primitive socialist accumulation." But it was he who had insisted that the increase in the peasants' ability to spend out of given income was the strongest single stimulant to "nonautonomous" investment; more importantly, no one stated more forcefully than he the ever-present danger of a peasants' strike in view of the lag in industrial supply. Such a danger could materialize during the "discontinuous reconstruction" when peasants were expected to give up more of their produce than before, while not getting correspondingly more in return (or more likely getting less). Preobrazhenski's celebrated directive: "Take from the petty bourgeois producers more than capitalism did [but] out of a [proportionally] still larger income," could hardly hold at this particular juncture. The "petty bourgeois producers" could respond to the attempt at an increased squeeze by withdrawing from the market, thus killing the industrial expansion by cutting off the supplies of food and, indirectly, of the foreign capital goods bought from the proceeds of agricultural exports. Or else, by forcing the state to capitulate, they could impose an increase in food prices and let the inflation start from this side. The cure would prove deadlier than the disease; this was, in effect, the point Preobrazhenski's opponents were making.

Preobrazhenski struggled vainly for a way out of this dilemma. . . .

. . . He concluded that "the sum total of these contradictions shows how strongly our development toward socialism is confronted with the necessity of ending our socialist isolation, not only for political but also for economic reasons, and of leaning for support in the future on the material resources of other socialist countries." At worst, this amounted to an admission that all attempts to find a solution within the limits of the isolated Soviet economy would be merely squaring the circle. At best, this was a desperate effort to obtain tomorrow's stability at the expense of enormously increased tensions today, without knowing too well how to withstand them.

It was not difficult for Preobrazhenski's opponents to prove that the "superindustrialist" way was leading to an impasse. To show a flaw in his reasoning was quite a different matter. Indeed, the main argument seemed ominously foolproof. The high rate of growth appeared as a vital necessity and at the same time as a threat. Granted the underlying assumptions, it was the case of a choice between mortal sickness and virtually certain death on the operating table.

. . . "Our economy," Bukharin declared, "exists for the consumer, and not the consumer for the economy." He praised this "new economy" which "differs from the old by taking as its guiding principle the needs of the masses and not the profit you are earning on Monday and Tuesday without thinking of what will happen on Thursday and Friday"; and he felt certain that the policy of keeping industrial prices down would force the plant managers to lower costs. At the same time, however, a new note crept into his pronouncements. He recognized that the Soviet economy was now facing a transition from the "period of restoration" to the "period of reconstruction." This assignment whose fulfillment "depends primarily upon our success in acquiring and applying capital . . . for the expansion of the basis of production, for the construction or the laying down of the new enterprises, to a considerable extent on a new technical basis" constituted "the task of greatest difficulty." . . .

. . . Bukharin and Rykov . . . were, no doubt, firmly convinced that the "American way" of combining a high rate of investment with a steady rise of the consumption levels of the urban and agricultural population could be emulated under the very different conditions of the Soviet economy of the twenties. The sum total of the policies outlined above, they felt, would be instrumental in bringing this about. But while the resolutions of the Fifteenth Congress spoke in ringing tones of confidence, their spiritual godfathers did not attempt to hide that the situation was bound to be touch and go for quite a while. True, they continued to insist that "we cannot and we must not choose the path of development at which the tasks of keeping up the highest possible tempo and of maintaining the moving equilibrium of the whole economic system exclude each other." But the significance of this statement was considerably reduced by the frank admission that "there is no guaranty" against "temporary imbalance" as long as there are no adequate reserves of raw materials, foodstuffs, finished goods, gold, etc. The building-up of such safety margins would be possible only by slowing down the tempo of capital construction — a policy which was now ruled out. It was therefore only logical for Rykov to declare that "if we want to develop heavy industry out of our own resources, and we must do it, we will have to retrench ourselves somewhat for a time." The "temporary excesses of demand over supply" were now accepted as well-nigh inevitable. The crucial task was to prevent them from reaching a level of "general economic crisis." The leaders of the Trotskyite opposition would find here little to disagree with. True, the left-wingers were still setting the "tempos" higher and were ready to rely in the main on the drastic levies imposed on the peasantry while the Bukharin-Rykov group preferred the methods of "repressed inflation." But these differences, important as they were, could not alter the fundamental fact that the former "harmonists" and the proponents of "primitive socialist accumulation" were by now solidly on the horns of the same dilemma, and none of them found this a comfortable position.

. . . Toward the end of the great debate the two main groups were much closer to each other than at its beginning: Bukharin and his followers admitted explicitly the inevitability of discontinuous growth, while Preobrazhenski became increasingly outspoken about the risks involved in such policy. It would not be unnatural to expect, under such circumstances, an attempt to work toward some middle ground.

Actual developments did not follow this path. The resolutions on economic policy adopted by the Fifteenth Congress of the CPSU could indeed be interpreted as a step toward a synthesis between the older right-wing and left-wing conceptions. However, this change of attitude had its corollary not in a rapprochement between the majority and the opposition, but in the crushing of the latter by force. All the leaders of the left wing, including Trotsky and Preobrazhenski, were expelled from the party. But this turn of events, however stunning, paled into insignificance in comparison with what came later. The "synthesis" went overboard within less than two years, and the new policy line which superseded it swung to extremes which the most ardent "superindustrializers" of the suppressed left wing had never imagined. The First Five Year Plan proclaimed as its objective an expansion in investment goods-output to the level which would make the fixed capital of the economy double within five years — a rate of growth unparalled in history. And while according to the professed intentions this expansion was to be accompanied by a marked increase in per capita consumption, in the process of actual fulfillment the first part of the program was pushed through unwaveringly at the expense of the second. . . .

. . . The rapid-fire industrialization and the sweeping collectivization were not merely devices of economic policy, but means of extending the direct control of the totalitarian state over the largest possible number within the shortest time. Yet the way in which this extension was brought about had, from the viewpoint of the "controllers," a high value of its own.

The lightning speed of the drive pulverized the will to resist. It whipped into enthusiastic action millions of young people yearning for heroic adventure. Last but not least, it succeeded in producing among many former stalwarts of the various intraparty oppositions the feeling that what had occurred was too far-reaching to be reversed without wrecking the whole social setup born of the revolution and that the thing to do under the circumstances was not to "rock the boat" but to close ranks in order to minimize the risks involved in the adopted policies.

It was this unique blend of creeping fear, exhilaration of battle, and *la-patrie-en-danger* psychosis that provided the intellectual climate for Stalin's "revolution from above." In such a climate there was no room for the ideas and concepts which have been presented on the pages of this study. We have seen the men who had defended them to be far apart in their initial blueprints, and even more — in the political premises on which these blueprints were based. But all of them — Left, Right, or Center — operated under the assumption that in the sphere of economic policy there are resistances of material which call not for a smashing knockout blow but for some kind of coexistence of heterogeneous socio-economic setups for a long time to come, with the result of an uneasy compromise shifting only gradually in the desired direction. They were more than once swayed in their reasoning by the emotions of political battle, in which quarter was neither asked nor given. Yet their basic ideas, as different from the occasional twists in their argument, reflected not the "ideological" juggling of facts and theoretical concepts but a genuine effort to come to grips with complex and intractable realities and to make the eventual solutions stand up against criticism. True, most of the participants in the great debate had been intellectually formed in the ranks of the Bolshevik old guard, which represented in the prerevolutionary period the authoritarian wing of Russian Marxism. But none of them succeeded any more than Lenin himself did in carrying through to its Stalinist perfection the basic attitudes toward man and society inherent in the elitist conception — the refusal to tolerate spheres of social life not fully manipulable from above, seeing weakness if not outright betrayal behind any diversity in thought and action, and the determination to use every means in order to stamp it out. It was the failure of Bukharin, Preobrazhenski, and others to live up to this totalitarian code that sealed their fate. All of them perished in the purges of the thirties.

The Struggle with the Right Opposition

ROBERT V. DANIELS

Stalin's struggle with the Right Opposition of Bukharin, Rykov, and Tomsky was the immediate prelude to the "Stalin Revolution" and the actual occasion for many of the new steps Stalin took. This episode has been studied in detail by the editor of the present collection of readings, as part of a history of all the Communist opposition factions from the Revolution to the triumph of Stalin. Much of the most revealing material on which this account is based, particularly the discussions at party meetings, comes from unpublished reports and minutes included among the papers which Trotsky brought out of Russia. These materials are now in the Trotsky Archive at Harvard University.

FOR all its affirmation of the virtue and necessity of monolithic unity, the Bolshevik Party could not yet dispense with the function provided by an opposition. Stalin and Bukharin had hardly finished congratulating themselves on their triumphant victory over the Trotskyists when a new party split began. In a matter of months, Stalin's senior associates in the Politburo — Bukharin, Rykov, and Tomsky — found themselves the victims of precisely the same political tactics whose use against the Left they had so vigorously applauded such a short time before.

The Right Opposition led by these three men was quite different in character from the previous Trotskyist movement. The Left oppositionists had exhibited a certain continuity of ideological tradition over a considerable span of years, and their disagreements with the Leninist leadership were substantially grounded in deep-seated intellectual and social differences. By contrast, the Right Opposition was a phenomenon of the moment, emerging on the political scene with little forewarning. The Right Opposition had no background as

a deviation, for the simple reason that before its appearance as an opposition it had been, both as a group of men and as a program, an indistinguishable part of the party leadership itself. In the form of its origin the Right Opposition thus closely resembled the Left Communists of 1918. Each group represented the previously prevailing line of the party from which the leading individual in the party suddenly swerved. In both instances the split thus produced was deep, and the manner in which the party crisis would be resolved was not immediately apparent. . . .

The pronouncements of the Fifteenth Congress were sufficiently vague to allow a variety of interpretations, as would soon become apparent. Indications are that the Stalinists still had no definite idea of the policy changes which they were soon to make, nor of the immediate economic and political problems which would force this shift. As usual in Soviet politics, the departure from the NEP and the new cleavage in the party were precipitated when expedients had to be devised to meet a sudden crisis.

Reprinted by permission of the publishers from Robert V. Daniels, *The Conscience of the Revolution: Communist Opposition in Soviet Russia.* Cambridge, Mass.: Harvard University Press, 1960 (Russian Research Center Studies, no. 40); Copyright by the President and Fellows of Harvard College. Pp. 322–324, 327–332, 337, 339–341, 348–352, 358–360.

The problem was a familiar one — the peasantry and the food supply. Even before the sessions of the Fifteenth Party Congress had been completed with the formal expulsion of the whole Left Opposition, the party leadership began to express alarm about grain procurement. Two directives issued from the Central Committee to local party organizations, warning of a decline in the collections of grain from the peasants. These were followed in January 1928 by an order threatening disciplinary action against local party leaders if they failed to remedy the situation. By February the entire party was agitated over the suddenly looming grain crisis. . . .

Despite the growing misgivings of many party figures, Stalin proceeded toward the statement of a basically new agricultural policy, though he disclaimed innovation by speaking of "implementing the decisions of the Fifteenth Congress." In a talk to a gathering of Communist scholars late in May, Stalin made public his new approach: "The solution lies in the transition from individual peasant farming to collective, common farming." He did make a gesture in the direction of improving individual farming while it lasted, but the toughness of his new orientation was reaffirmed in his comment on industry: "Should we, perhaps, as a measure of greater 'caution,' retard the development of heavy industry and make light industry, which produces chiefly for the peasant market, the basis of our industry as a whole? Not under any circumstances! That would be suicidal; it would mean undermining our whole industry, including light industry. It would mean the abandonment of the slogan of the industrialization of our country, and the transformation of our country into an appendage of the capitalist system of economy." Here Stalin announced what was to become the main theme of the economic discussions and controversies of the ensuing year. He had opted for the high-tempo industrialization which had just been condemned along with the Left Opposition, and he went even further with his refusal to recognize any limits either on the country's need for heavy industry or on its capacity for building it.

Bukharin's first response to the new stress on collectivization was a panegyric on the "cultural revolution," which would put an end to "the contrast of city and country," but soon he removed his rose-colored glasses. By the first of June, Bukharin had privately attacked Stalin as the representative of a "Trotskyist danger," and he soon became the leading spokesman for a determined though still behind-the-scenes faction committed to the defeat of Stalin's line on agriculture. . . .

By the time of the July meeting of the Central Committee, rumors of dissension in the highest councils of the party were rife. Trotsky took note of "the existing breach between the apparatus and the right wing," although the make-up of the latter was not entirely clear to him. Stalin apparently contemplated some kind of drastic action, though he may not yet have been sure of its precise direction.

Among Stalin's potential supporters and critics the lines had not definitely formed. Molotov spoke on June 30 with weighty caution, stressing the burden of backwardness in Russian agriculture and warning against excessive reliance on planning alone. At the same meeting, Uglanov, who was about to take the Moscow organization into the Right Opposition, expressed precisely the opposite, optimistic, view of planning. Earlier, Kaganovich had supposedly wavered. Kalinin, Voroshilov, Andreiyev, Ordzhonikidze, and the deputy GPU [1] chief, Yagoda, among others, were rumored to be sympathetic toward Stalin's opponents. They were reportedly afraid to act or restrained by

[1] GPU or OGPU: The "Chief Political Administration" or "United Chief Political Administration," the political police (originally the "Cheka" or "Extraordinary Commission to Combat Counter-Revolution"; later the "NKVD" or "People's Commissariat of Internal Affairs"; now the "KGB" or "Committee of State Security"). [Editor's note.]

threats of blackmail by Stalin. Voroshilov, for example, apparently feared the exposure of his sin of patriotic fervor which prompted him to volunteer for the tsarist army during World War I.

The Central Committee assembled for its regular meeting in Moscow on July 4. Again the focus of its deliberations was the peasant problem, which was the subject of a climactic debate on July 9 and 10. Reports were delivered by Kalinin, Molotov, and Mikoyan, dealing respectively with state farms, collective farms, and grain collections; they spoke in relatively moderate terms, with emphasis on maintaining the tie with the middle peasant. The principal resolution, proposed by Mikoyan, was a compromise document which stressed the need for raising the productivity of individual peasant farming, underscored the temporary nature of the extraordinary measures, and even admitted the necessity of raising the price of grain to correspond with the price of other agricultural products. It was, in fact, essentially Bukharin's resolution, "stolen from my declaration," as he put it.

Mikoyan's presentation was the signal for a series of right-wing comments, by Osinsky, Andreyev, A. I. Stetsky, and Sokolnikov, that the agricultural situation was still serious and that further concessions to the middle peasants (especially price increases) were imperative. Uglanov and Rykov followed with warnings about the general state of popular discontent and the danger of allowing the extraordinary measures to become an accepted system. Kaganovich entered the argument to protest that the extraordinary measures had been criticized too much, and that it was equally wrong to rely wholly on price policy. Some of his remarks were the harshest heard at the plenum: "The kulak's[2] struggle with us will be cruel. . . . We must prepare for this. We must quicken the pace of the grain collection campaign." Rykov replied emotionally to Kaganovich, "It would be wrong to make a distinction between the extraordinary measures and 'excesses.' 'Excesses' sometimes include criminal or semicriminal offenses committed by individual persons in the process of collecting grain. This is altogether wrong. A crime is a crime. A whole series of 'excesses' was an organic part of the entire system of grain collections which we resorted to in January." Kaganovich, according to Rykov, was an apologist for violence as an end in itself: "The whole meaning of Kaganovich's speech reduces to the defense of extraordinary measures as such for any time and under any conditions." Kaganovich was "cut to pieces," in Sokolnikov's estimation.

Stalin took part in the discussion with a major speech on July 9. His point of departure was the Osinsky-Sokolnikov price-raising proposal, which he denounced as "putting the brakes on the industrialization of the country." By concentrating his fire against the most extreme representatives of the right-wing view (whom Rykov himself repudiated), Stalin endeavored to identify their heresy with all the opposition to his own view. The substance of Stalin's speech was to give the NEP a new meaning — it was not a retreat but an offensive, in which vigorous measures against the kulaks and the collectivization of the rest of the peasants had an appropriate place. Thus, in his usual fashion, Stalin was able to indulge himself in a new policy and still profess orthodox adherence to past authority. He anticipated objections to accelerated collectivization by classing them with opposition to the collectivist goal per se: "Those who fail to understand that, or who do not want to admit it, are not Marxists or Leninists, but peasant philosophers, looking backward instead of forward."

Stalin took pains to distinguish his new policy from the Trotskyist program, with which many people had naturally associ-

[2] "Kulak": a prosperous individual peasant, from the Russian word for "fist," i.e., "tight-fisted." [Editor's note.]

ated it. In fact he was moving rapidly toward the Left position and was soon to go far beyond it with the initiation of violent, rapid, and wholesale collectivization of the peasants. Trotsky took note of a Rightist hope that a fear of conceding the correctness of the Left would inhibit the Stalinists in changing their policy. But Stalin again evidenced that doctrinal adroitness which belies the impression that he was clumsy and unlettered in matters of theory. His interest in theory was, to be sure, primarily a weapon to use against his enemies, but he wielded it with dexterity. As Bukharin confided to Kamenev, "Stalin . . . is an unprincipled intriguer who subordinates everything to the preservation of his power. He changes his theories according to whom he needs to get rid of at any given moment."

Stalin's problem in the summer of 1928 was to borrow the Leftist policy of increased pressure on the peasants without appearing to adhere to the Trotskyist heresy. At the same time he was determined to maneuver those who held to the old official policy into a position where they appeared to be deviators. Bukharin complained, "He maneuvers in such a way as to make us stand as the schismatics." Stalin's strategy for accomplishing these simultaneous feats of political sleight of hand was his usual redefinition of old party clichés, with the support of appropriately culled quotations from Lenin, to make accepted ideas mean something quite different. At the same time his firm adherence to the authoritative pronouncements of the party would be loudly proclaimed, and anyone who ventured to suggest divergence in the actual application of such pronouncements would immediately find himself charged with an un-Leninist attitude. So it was with those who complained that the actual trend of peasant policy was violating the spirit of the NEP. They were dismissed as a "kulak deviation."

On July 10, as recriminations between the factions at the Central Committee plenum grew increasingly bitter, Bukharin rose to make the major statement of his case. He was in deadly earnest, throughout frequent clownish heckling by the Stalinists, and sincerely alarmed over the security of the Soviet state, which he feared was threatened by a mass uprising under the leadership of the kulaks. "To undertake the slightest campaign in the country," he warned "means to mobilize against us to an ever greater degree the kulak element, the petty bourgeoisie . . . the middle bourgeoisie . . . etc. The reserves of these forces remain very great, and the slightest vacillation on the question in the ranks of our party will have a disproportionately great political significance."

The grain crisis, Bukharin explained, was a reflection of the country's basic economic weakness: reserves were seriously lacking, and it was proving impossible to advance simultaneously in agriculture, industry, and consumer satisfaction. "Give us your panacea," interjected Voroshilov, who was at pains to demonstrate by his repeated heckling of Bukharin that he sided firmly with the Stalinists.

"I don't want to give you a panacea, and please don't you make fun of me," replied Bukharin, stung by the remark but apparently unable to grasp the factional vindictiveness of his critics. He went on to criticize Stalin for suggesting that industrial development inevitably implied a threat to the worker-peasant alliance: this was a Trotskyist notion. It was wrong to attack reliance on price measures as capitalistic: prices were the decisive means whereby the government could regulate the individual peasants. Poor planning and incorrect pricing were responsible for the crisis that required such special measures. The extraordinary measures had tended to become a system of War Communism; their economic value was questionable and their political effect was indisputably bad. At all costs the allegiance of the middle peasants had to be kept, and this meant that their individual farms should be allowed to prosper more. The offensive against the kulaks could be continued, but only in the form of exploiting their productive capacity through taxation; the kulaks would be no threat as long as the middle peasants did not decide to follow them. Conciliation of the peasants was the key to the future — "We must in no case allow a threat to the smychka." [3]

The compromise resolution on the grain collections was passed unanimously by the Central Committee after the close of debate on July 10. It gave many people the impression that the issues between the Stalinists and the Rykov-Bukharin group had been completely settled. The shifting balance was subtly revealed, however, where the resolution condemned the Rightists' principal complaint that the extraordinary measures were becoming an established policy: "Interpretations of these measures as organic consequences of the decisions of the Fifteenth Congress . . . testify only to the fact that at certain levels of the party an alien ideology has had influence." The Rightist leaders discovered that their position was crumbling, as a number of the people on whom they thought they could count — including Voroshilov, Kalinin, and Kuibyshev — lined up on Stalin's side. Stalin's attitude on July 11, the last day of the session, was correspondingly tougher. The general secretary was confidently unyielding about suggestions for further leniency toward the peasantry.

Stalin's opponents now decided to act. It is not hard to imagine how their feelings took form — after enthusiastic collaboration with a strong and resourceful comrade, the growing discord, the verbal altercation when unleashed tempers turned uneasy friends into vengeful enemies, the nursing of grudges and the restrained growling in public encounters, and finally the horrifying realization that the old associate was a power-hungry in-

triguer who now held most of the cards and would stop at nothing in his determination to destroy them. While reports flew about that the Right was planning to depose Stalin, Bukharin took the risky step of establishing contact with former members of the Left Opposition. Sokolnikov arranged a meeting between Bukharin and Kamenev. For some reason Bukharin had come to fear a rapprochement between Stalin and the Zinoviev-Kamenev group, and he hastened to seek out the old oppositionists to be his own allies on the ground that they had a common cause to make.

On the morning of July 11, Sokolnikov and Bukharin slipped into Kamenev's Moscow apartment without ringing, and Bukharin, in a desperate mood, at once revealed his fears: "Stalin's line is ruinous for the whole revolution. It can make us collapse. . . . The differences between us and Stalin are many times more serious than all our former differences with you. Rykov, Tomsky, and I agree on formulating the situation thus: 'It would be much better if Zinoviev and Kamenev were in the Politburo instead of Stalin.' . . . I have not spoken with Stalin for several weeks. . . . Our arguing with him reached the point of saying, 'You lie!' He has made concessions now, so that [later] he can cut our throats." In the comments which he appended to the record of the talk, Kamenev observed, "Stalin knows only one method . . . to plant a knife in your back."

* * *

The scene of the organizational struggle between Stalin and the Right was Moscow. The party machine in the Moscow province was the only major organizational force at the disposal of the Rightists and accordingly was of strategic significance. In contrast to the spontaneous and relatively democratic surge of Opposition sentiment among the Moscow Communists in 1923 and earlier, the 1928 Moscow Opposition was an apparatus af-

[3] Smychka: the supposed "bond" or alliance between the workers and the peasants. [Editor's note.]

fair, on the order of Zinoviev's Leningrad Opposition of 1925. Uglanov's Moscow Opposition was no more a democratic protest movement than was Stalin's central party machine. Uglanov was a typical organization man, installed in the key Moscow post in 1924 and rewarded for his loyalty to the general secretary by elevation to the Politburo as a candidate member in 1925.

The fact that a man such as Uglanov should have thrown his lot in with the Bukharin group indicates that the issues between Stalin and the Right had driven a deep wedge into the ranks of the party officialdom. While the motive of personal political advantage cannot be ruled out, Uglanov's stand during and after the July Plenum of the Central Committee leaves no doubt that he was genuinely concerned over economic policy and that he took the Bukharinist alarm to heart. Like the other Rightist leaders, he linked the success of the Communist Party with the well-being of the country and recoiled before the social conflict which Stalin's aggressive line portended. . . .

The central party leadership . . . proceeded to deal with the Opposition in Moscow with the usual organizational measures. Under the convenient pretext provided by the current campaigns for "self-criticism" and "intraparty democracy," and utilizing the scheduled elections for new bureaus or directing committees for all party cells, the Stalinists by-passed the Moscow leadership in order to apply pressure and seek supporters in the district organizations nominally under the jurisdiction of the Moscow Committee. "It is true" the Central Committee announced, "that some members of the Moscow Committee and the leaders of some districts have recently shown a certain inconsistency and vacillation in the struggle against the Right deviations from the Leninist line by tolerating a conciliatory attitude toward these deviations which is inacceptable to the Bolshevik Party. This has aroused the dissatisfac-

tion of a certain section of the active membership of the Moscow organization who wished to correct these mistakes." Here were the tactics employed so effectively against the Zinovievists in Leningrad in January 1926. They demonstrated the top leadership's ability to go outside the normal lines of bureaucratic authority and make use of democratic forms in order to buttress central control over the middle echelons.

Soon there were subtle indications of the effect of central pressure. Some of the Moscow district organizations, passing resolutions about the Comintern congress, began to express the new central line against "petty-bourgeois opportunism" in the Russian party itself. Other Moscow districts confined themselves to vague exhortations for the "struggle on two fronts." As it was later officially confirmed, the district secretaries had divided in their allegiance between Uglanov and the central leadership. The party organization at Moscow University, reflecting the intellectuals' predilection for any form of opposition, took a firm pro-Rightist stand.

To appease the central leadership, Uglanov issued a declaration to the Moscow membership early in October, in which he heavily stressed the danger of the Right deviation as well as the Left. But he did not put an end to the tolerance of Rightist opinions within his organization and lamely had to plead the "sickness" of himself and his two co-secretaries as the excuse. Uglanov was evidently encouraged by the publication of Bukharin's thoughtful critique of the Stalinist economic program, his "Notes of an Economist," in *Pravda* on September 30. On October 3 he warned publicly that Soviet agriculture was now seriously lagging, to the detriment of both industry and consumers. On the following day, one of Uglanov's district secretaries, Penkov, echoed these agriculture-first remarks and urged the study of Bukharin's article, but he met with an ominous response —

direct contradiction by his own subordinates in the debate which ensued.

On or about October 11, the central leadership initiated a violent press and organizational campaign against the still anonymous "Right deviation," and simultaneously took direct action against the Moscow Opposition. Uglanov suddenly found that he could no longer control transfers in his own organization. While the bureau of the Moscow Committee was compelled to share responsibility for the move, it was on the acknowledged initiative of the Central Committee that the two most recalcitrant district leaders in Moscow, Penkov and Riutin, were removed, on the grounds that they had "recently allowed individual deviations from the correct Leninist line of the party." Confirmation of the central victory came at the meeting of the Moscow Committee on October 18 and 19. Uglanov made the customary report but was given a portent of his coming fall as the committee members withheld the usual applause. Sensing the forces against him, Uglanov remarked ironically that his removal would be justified if the membership really wanted it. He admitted weaknesses in his organization and vaguely conceded "lack of clarity in evaluating the economic situation," but he tried to stand his ground against the Stalinists' attacks: "We will consider it our duty . . . to defend ourselves by struggling against slander." Guardedly he recalled Lenin's warning about Stalin's character.

Uglanov's defensive gestures were fruitless, for the great majority of the Moscow Committee had evidently gone over to the Stalinists. The proceedings of the session were largely taken up with criticism of Uglanov's errors, attacks on the Right deviation, and appeals for discipline and self-criticism. The oppositionists were accused of a "keep it in the family" attitude and of conniving against the Central Committee. A number of Uglanov's supporters, including the ousted district secretaries Penkov and Riutin, made their confessions and boarded the band wagon. "The party is *exclusively* correct," declared district secretary Safronov, "and I find in myself enough courage to admit my errors." A hold-out, the dismissed agitprop chief Liadov-Mandelshtam, pleaded that his friends had no honor because they avoided him as "a traitor to the party line."

On October 19 Stalin appeared in person before the Moscow Committee to deliver a long warning against the Right deviation, though he still allowed it to remain anonymous. Affirming that a Right deviation did in fact exist among the Russian Communists as well as in the Comintern, he described it as "a tendency, an inclination of a part of the Communists, not yet formulated, it is true, and perhaps not yet consciously realized, but nevertheless a tendency, to depart from the general line of our party toward bourgeois ideology." This was not, Stalin argued, a new development, but it had been revealed more clearly by the "vacillations" which the government's recent economic problems had produced. Cleverly he twisted the Rightist efforts to defend the old party line and created an antiproletarian scapegoat: "In order to overcome the difficulties we must first defeat the Right danger . . . which is hindering the fight against our difficulties and is trying to shake the party's will to fight to overcome these difficulties."

. . . Uglanov's resistance collapsed completely in the face of the general secretary's attack. The Moscow Committee confessed the "mistake" in its work and approved without reservation the removals which had been ordered by the Central Committee. The disgrace of Uglanov was confirmed by his subordinates' criticizing him to his face for "insufficient" recognition of his "errors." . . .

While Stalin was destroying the foothold of the Right Opposition in the party organization and in the trade unions, the policy cleavage between his forces and the Right grew wider. From the specific issue of the kulaks and the grain problem the controversy broadened to include the most general problems of economic life and the country's future prospects. Ramifications of the controversy reached to the core of Marxian doctrine and into the most abstruse philosophical matters.

The political origins of the industrialization policy formulated by the Stalinists late in 1928 are abundantly clear when the problem is viewed in the context of the debates of 1925–1927. The issues were essentially the same, with the Stalinists taking the position of Preobrazhensky and the Trotskyists, against the Rightists who adhered to the earlier official position. Stalin's new affinity with the former Leftist program of intensive planned industrialization at the expense of the peasantry was only emphasized by the vigorous efforts which he made to refute the insinuation that he was merely copying the Trotskyist policy two years too late. (As late as November 1928, the charge "super-industrialist" was still being hurled at the Trotskyists.) The "capitulations" of exiled Trotskyists who decided that Stalin's program was close enough to their own show clearly enough how the new line actually appeared. In part, Stalin's espousal of the Leftist program was an acknowledgment of the country's economic impasse as the Left Opposition had analyzed it. His immediate interest in industrialization, however, was mainly political. It was a device to provoke the Rightists into making protests that could be called deviation.

While the Right-Left political battle raged in 1926 and 1927 over the speed of industrialization, a parallel cleavage developed among the professional economists. Two distinct conceptions of the nature of planning had emerged by 1927, represented respectively by the "geneticists" and the "teleologists." The geneticists stressed the work of predicting uncontrollable economic tendencies, and adapting plans accordingly, while the teleologists argued that the laws of eco-

nomics could be transcended by the action of the socialist state. "Our task is not to study economics but to change it," wrote the leading professional exponent of the latter view, S. G. Strumilin, in a paraphrase of Marx. "We are bound by no laws. There are no fortresses which Bolsheviks cannot storm" — a slogan which Stalin was later to plagiarize. "The question of tempo is subject to decision by human beings." . . .

While Gosplan [the State Planning Commission] wrestled with the formulation of a plan that would take all such contingencies [as defects of organization and accounting, and the uncertainties of the harvest and of foreign trade conditions] into account, a rival organization was moving into the planning field. This was the Supreme Economic Council (which actually functioned as the commissariat of industry), headed since 1926 by Kuibyshev, the former chairman of the Central Control Commission and a dedicated, if somewhat colorless, Stalinist. Under Kuibyshev, the Supreme Economic Council proceeded to draw up its own drafts of a five-year plan, with considerably more emphasis on heavy industry. "Castles in air," scoffed the Gosplan economists. . . .

Kuibyshev's speech to the Leningrad party organization on September 19 was the firmest declaration yet heard of a determination to drive ahead and to eliminate any discontent engendered by the drive. "We must be fully aware," Kuibyshev asserted, "that it would be wrong from every point of view to speak of a reduction of the rate of industrialization. . . . We are told we are 'overindustrializing,' and 'biting off more than we can chew.'" This was a patent reference to the warnings from the Bukharin-Rykov group — but the objection was overruled: "Any careful student of our economy will, I am sure, agree with me that the most serious disproportion . . . is the one between the output of the means of production and the requirements of the country." The vindication of Preobrazhensky could not have been more explicit. . . .

The reflection of the party split in the work of economic planning reached the point of crisis in the winter of 1928–29. The right-wing Gosplan could not overcome its scruples and repeatedly failed to give the party leadership what was wanted, while the Supreme Economic Council went forging ahead with ever more optimistic visions. "Our planning," read a statement of the latter organization, "must include not only forecasting, not only the discovery of economic laws, but a creative, deliberate building of a socialist economy." This was the teleological approach with a vengeance.

At the end of November 1928, too late for the Central Committee to act upon it, the planners in the Supreme Economic Council finally produced an optimal five-year plan which was acceptable to the leadership. The draft had been completed under such pressure for haste that Kuibyshev was unable to carry out his promise to go through the motions of "mass participation" in the preparation of the plan. According to this new version, industrial investment would not only be undertaken at a high rate, but the percentage of the national income devoted to it would increase, year after year, through the five-year period. The party leadership immediately turned, for a convenient forum, to the Eighth Trade Union Congress, and Kuibyshev appeared there to expound at great length the virtues of the new plan, which excluded all previous versions — "Only this variant can be placed under consideration." Brought to heel by party pressure, the trade-unionists gave their endorsement to the plan. Gosplan still remained critical. Bazarov warned, with courage that was remarkable at this late date, "Here there can be the worst results, here you can get such a clearly irrational distribution of resources as will discredit the whole idea of industrialization."

By the early months of 1929, the party leadership was locked in bitter controversy with Bukharin, Rykov, and Tomsky. The Stalinists became unalterably committed to the highest conceivable speed of economic development, if only to assure that the right would be branded as fainthearted deviators. At the same time they accused the Rightist critics of playing politics — compunctions about economic equilibrium were dismissed as "a mere convenient screen for political rather than methodological attacks."

In the meantime, the uncooperative economists were disposed of. Quietly but thoroughly Gosplan was purged; everyone associated with the geneticist position was ousted. The planning efforts already accomplished were rejected for following the "wrong class approach," and the party leadership proclaimed the exclusive orthodoxy of the "purposive-teleological method." A number of the former Gosplan economists, especially those who had originally been associated with the Mensheviks,[4] were involved on charges of "sabotage" in the "Industrial Party" trial of 1930 and the Menshevik trial of 1931. But the shake-up did not stop here. The Stalinist drive for heavy industrial development transcended even what the teleological economists thought feasible, and they in their turn were thrust aside into academic positions. . . .

In March 1929, the renovated Gosplan finally produced a full-dress plan with two complete variants. The times were changing fast, however; Kuibyshev now replied, "The optimal variant of the five-year plan is the plan for building socialism." The Rightists protested and vainly proposed alternatives—Rykov suggested a "middle variant" and a subsidiary two-year program for agriculture. This brought down on him the charge that he opposed the five-year plan and defended the kulaks.

[4] Mensheviks: The more moderate wing of the Russian Marxists, who had opposed Lenin and the Bolsheviks since 1903. [Editor's note.]

The First Five Year Plan was finally approved as official party policy at the Sixteenth Party Conference in April 1929, and confirmed in May by the Council of People's Commissars and the Congress of Soviets. The new optimal variant was declared to have been in effect as of October of the previous year. The role of chance was dismissed by governmental decree. Any concern for such bothersome economic considerations as statistical relationships or laws of equilibrium was swept aside as "class-alien." The new mentality was epitomized in the slogan, "There are no objective obstacles — obstacles must be overcome." Speaking at the Seventeenth Party Congress in 1934, Stalin declared that "objective conditions" could no longer be admitted as factors limiting the will of the Soviet government. Henceforth, there was no excuse for failure — treason could be the only explanation.

Ideological Revision

RAYMOND A. BAUER

The New Man in Soviet Psychology, by Raymond A. Bauer (1916–   ), Professor of Industrial Psychology at the Harvard Business School, is a survey of psychological thought in Soviet Russia during the first twenty years after the revolution. Professor Bauer found it necessary to clarify the ideological background of Soviet psychology, and in so doing he produced a challenging explanation of Stalin's use of Marxist theory. Marxism was no longer to be understood as a mechanistic theory of the inevitable laws of economic change. Instead, with emphasis on the "dialectic," Marxism was interpreted as "purposive," to justify the ambitions of Stalin's government and the requirements imposed on the Soviet citizens. Any adherence to the older Marxist view was henceforth outlawed as a "bourgeois" sentiment.

STALIN has stressed the activist element in Leninism. He cited, for example, Lenin's opposition to the theory of "spontaneity" on the ground that reliance on the elemental forces in the social process undermined the active role of the Party. Stalin has said that if the interpretation of social processes held by some groups at the beginning of the century had been accepted there would have been no need "for an independent working class party." He suggests a mock conversation with a person who overemphasizes the importance of relying on spontaneous forces. Suppose, he queries, you were to ask such a person what the role of the Party should be.

"What are you talking about?" comes the ready answer.

"Can the Party do anything to affect the working of so decisive a factor as 'the level of the forces of production'?"

Thus, the Party, in the eyes of such a person can have no effective role in shaping history.

Lenin, says Stalin, revived the revolutionary aspects of Marxism, which had been played down by the moderate socialists, and in addition adapted Marxism to the demands of modern conditions: "It is a fact that Lenin brought to light once more the revolutionary social content of Marxism, which had been glossed over by the opportunists of the Second International, but that is only a fragment of the truth. The whole truth is that Leninism is a development of Marxism adapting it to the new conditions of capitalism and to the class struggle of the proletariat." Thus Stalin places himself and Lenin firmly on the side of those who favor action rather than rely on the determinate course of events.

For particular historical reasons the question of determinism and freedom has been a central problem in the development of Marxist-Leninist thought and action. All social action — and implicitly all social theory — involves some compromise between determinacy and indeterminacy, some judgment of the extent to which one is free to act and the extent to which one is constrained by circumstance. As practical experience has made the limitations of circumstances more explicit, an ever greater emphasis has had to be placed on the power of the individual to act in such a way as to overcome these limitations. This condition evolved because early predictions based on assumed determinate relationships gave a sanguine picture of the trend of social developments — thus minimizing the emphasis which had to be placed on the role of the individual — whereas later predictions forecast conditions which could not be accepted — therefore necessitating reliance on individual action to negate the trend of determined (that is, predicted) events. An optimism based on predicted immanent developments became replaced with an "optimism" based on man's ability to make his own fate. It is not true that in every instance early predictions were optimistic and later predictions were pessimistic. It is true, however, that a particular set of

early "optimistic" predictions about the withering away of the state and about the nature of socialist institutions were not realized, and it is also true that the relative weight to be assigned to "spontaneous," or determinate and noncontrolled, forces in a situation was a recurrent question in problem after problem.

The social postulates of extreme mechanistic Marxism certainly include the following: (1) Man is a product of his inheritance and his environment; therefore society is responsible for man's character and behavior, rather than man's being responsible for society. (2) All social events are determinately related; therefore the trend of future events can be predicted. (3) Essentially, the course of events is determined by abstract forces external to man himself, and there is little that he could or should do to direct them. (4) Since all oppressive and repressive institutions are a function of conflict in class society, a classless society will speedily do away with repression. (5) Class society is a result of a particular form of economic relations, and a change in the economic base of society will eliminate class divisions, which in turn will result in the withering away of the state and bring about ideal social conditions. (6) Man is inherently rational and inherently good; and once he is freed from the institutions of a class society, he will revert spontaneously to rationality and goodness. In addition to these premises, mechanistic Marxism posits the desirability of a freely developed and fully expressed personality, of freeing man from excessive burdens and of respecting his dignity.

Many of the premises involved in this type of thinking, and in fact some of the specific postulates outlined above, could be found in the work of virtually every Bolshevik at one time or another, and they found expression briefly in most of the Soviet social institutions. However, as the history of the Soviet Union unfolded, it became evident that these postulates were untenable in various areas of society, and factions began to develop on the basis of whether they gave predominant emphasis to the determinate trend of events or to the shaping of these events to a given goal. What had been a conflict in the minds of men became a conflict between men of different minds.

The conflict between these two sets of postulates was resolved in two critical events. The first was a crisis in economic planning in connection with the First Five Year Plan, and the second, a controversy between the mechanists and the dialecticians in philosophy. Beginning independently, these two events converged in the late twenties to precipitate a series of parallel crises in other areas of Soviet life. . . .

Two broad methodological issues were at stake. The first of which, as Bukharin himself put it in the early thirties, after accepting the defeat of his position, was between two orders of lawfulness: the lawfulness of events impinging on each other and working out their own resolution, and the lawfulness of events consciously organized and directed by man. The second issue involved the nature of evolution in general. The mechanistic conception of evolution or development sees events as proceeding linearly and sees the future as a direct projection of the past. The other point of view sees evolution as a discontinuous course of development involving periods of crisis and revolution producing sudden basic reorganizations of the elements in the system. This results in a new form of organization, subject to different laws — the dialectical law of quantity changing into quality. According to the dialectical point of view an accelerated program of industrialization and collectivization would produce such a "leap" in development and would result in restructuring of social relationships that would negate the predictions of the mechanists.

Further, the supporters of Stalin said that merchanists had no place for chance (accident) in their scheme of thinking. "They undertook a mystical view that

everything was defined by preceding events. For this, we inevitably slip down to fatalism in practice, to an excuse for abandoning the revolutionary fight, for reaction and all subjective errors. This mechanistic necessity forces us to dig in the past, seeking there the causes of the actual event, to look — not forward, but — backward." In other words, the Right opportunist has used scientific analysis to make man the slave rather than the master of events.

The victory of the Stalinist position had a number of important consequences for the future of Soviet society. (1) The primacy of "teleological" over "genetic" considerations was established in economic and social planning. There was, in effect, a basic redefinition — or clarification — of man's relation to his environment. It made official the view that man is the master of his own fate. (2) The controversy in planning crystallized the controversy in philosophy by underscoring the practical implications of the contesting philosophical positions. Under the pressure of the fight over the Five Year Plan, the "dialectical" position became clarified, and was established as the "correct" Marxist (Stalinist) philosophy. This, in turn, meant that dialectical materialism (as opposed to mechanistic materialism) became the accepted methodology of science. (3) The scope of the Plan itself precipitated a series of social crises, social needs, and problems which set their own chain of causation working. Social institutions (some soon, some late) became more tightly integrated, more explicitly directed toward the service of specific functions. Demands on and opportunities for the individual increased. At the same time the government actually had to be stricter in its control of the individual because of the large number of persons — kulaks, nepmen, and so on — against whom it had taken action. It also had to demand more of the individual in the service of the rapidly expanding economy.

The period of the twenties in Soviet

Russia was marked by an extended controversy in science and philosophy over the relative merits of dialectical and mechanistic materialism. There were actually two prongs to the discussion. One issue was whether or not the principles of dialectics, part of the official Marxist philosophy, were applicable to the natural sciences. The other issue was the actual definition of the principles of dialectics. . . .

The victory of the dialecticians was announced in April 1929, the same month in which Bukharin and other members of the Right opposition were stripped of much of their political power. The Second All-Union Conference of Marxist-Leninist Scientific Institutions passed a resolution labeling the view of the mechanists "a clear departure from the Marxist-Leninist philosophical position" and stating that "the theoretical discussion with the mechanists is really finished." Shortly after this the Central Committee of the Party issued a decree instructing the Communist Academy to implement the introduction of the dialectical point of view in the natural sciences. . . .

. . . What is significant in this philosophical discussion is that in each instance the dialecticians chose the point of view that left the Party free to act in reconstructing society and provided a rationale for holding the individual responsible for his behavior.

Fighting out the battles of everyday practical politics and economics in so scholarly an arena as philosophy may seem somewhat out of place to anyone not versed in the history of Bolshevism, but it was standard procedure in the Bolshevik manual of tactics to use every weapon available, from the most prosaic to the most esoteric.

Consider the situation in which the philosophical controversy reached its peak. Stalin was coming into ascendancy as the leader of the Party. While by no means handicapped by an inferior intellect, he had neither stature nor experience as a theorist. But he is and was a man of far

more than average shrewdness and common sense, who realized that the Soviet Union had reached a crisis. At the same time he was maneuvering for position with contending factions in the Party. It seems to have become obvious to Stalin about 1928 that the program of the Left, which had been rejected two years before, was originally correct, or that the situation had changed so that the Leftist program either had to be or could be put into effect. In any event, he espoused essentially the program of industrial expansion that the Left had originally proposed, and then found himself opposed by the "learned arguments" of the newly developed Right opposition. Without considering the merits of the two positions, we know that there were substantial temperamental differences between men like Nikolai Bukharin and Michael Tomsky, on the one hand, and Stalin and his supporters, on the other. The latter group were primarily men of direct action, men who favored active intervention to passive waiting. They were, further, men who were used to bending philosophy to the service of action. The position of the dialecticians offered a way out of the dilemma of determinism, of escaping from a fatalistically determined course of history. Also, the arguments of the dialecticians were a powerful weapon against the theories of Stalin's chief remaining competition, the Party's leading thinker, Bukharin. Thus, by force of circumstance, the least theoretically minded of Bolshevik leaders seems to have become the sponsor of one of the most sophisticated and possibly the most sophistic of theories. . . .

Beyond affirming the purposive nature of man, the establishment of the "Leninist line" in philosophy amounted to a very strong statement of the necessity for "a unity of theory and practice" in all science. The latter point is of primary concern here.

The slogan of the "unity of theory and

practice — with practice leading theory" is integrally related in Bolshevik thinking with the idea of *partinost*, literally "Partyness," which can best be translated as "Party vigilance" or "political acuity in the interest of the Party." The principle of political vigilance means that every citizen must always be alert to sense the implications of any theory or action from the point of view of the political program of the Party, and that the "truth" of any theory or the value of any action is determined on the basis of whether or not it contributes to the Party's program.

It is typical of the Bolshevik system that such a highly political, virtually anti-intellectual approach to science is based in a very sophisticated manner on a highly intellectual foundation, Lenin's theory of epistomology.

As developed by Soviet theoreticians after 1930, the essential point in Lenin's theory of knowledge (known in Soviet literature as the Leninist theory of reflection) is that there is an *absolute* truth, but that at any point in time man knows only relative truth, and that he knows this relative truth by virtue of his action on the real world. Absolute truth is approached by successive approximations as each partial truth is discarded and revised in the light of man's attempt to apply it in practice. However, the nature of man's activity, the nature of his understanding of the real world is conditioned by the social order in which he lives, and by his class membership in that order. Every theory is conditioned by *and* serves the interest of some social class. (Note the conjunctive *and;* the fallacy in the argument which follows hinges on the addition of the second verb in the sentence.) Membership in any social class places limitations on one's ability to perceive reality as it is. But the further advanced in the historical sequence any class is, the better equipped its members are to know reality. Each successive order of society permits its members to approach more closely absolute truth, and the most advanced type of society, socialist society, in which the proletarian class (the only class which is not blinded by prejudices and rationalizations) rules, creates the most favorable conditions for discovering truth. Since all truth is relative and serves some class interest, and since the proletarian class has the closest approximation of truth, thus the theory which serves the interest of the proletariat is the closest approximation to absolute truth. Therefore, the primary criterion for validating a scientific theory is the exercise of "party vigilance." A theory is true if it serves the interests of the proletariat, or, more accurately, the vanguard of the proletariat, the Bolshevik Party.

II. THE ECONOMIC REVOLUTION

The Socialist Drive

J. V. STALIN

Joseph Vissarionovich Stalin (1879–1953) rose from humble beginnings in a worker's family (real name Dzhugashvili) in the Transcaucasian region of Georgia, to become General Secretary of the Russian Communist Party in 1922 and unchallenged dictator of the Soviet Union in 1929. During the middle part of his career — from the mid-1920's to the mid-1930's — he recorded his achievements and intentions extensively in his many speeches, the most important of which were collected and translated in the various editions of *Problems of Leninism*. In speeches of November and December, 1929, Stalin set forth a résumé of the new industrial and agricultural policies he had initiated. In Stalin's mind there were only two possibilities — his own policy, "forward — to Socialism," or the retreat to capitalism which he charged his Communist opponents with advocating.

THE past year witnessed a great change on all fronts of Socialist construction. The change expressed itself, and is still expressing itself, in a determined *offensive* of Socialism against the capitalist elements in town and country. The characteristic feature of this offensive is that it has already brought us a number of decisive *successes,* in the principal spheres of the Socialist reconstruction of our national economy.

We may therefore conclude that our Party has made good use of the retreat effected during the first stages of the New Economic Policy in order to organize the *change* in the subsequent stages and to launch a *successful offensive* against the capitalist elements.

When the New Economic Policy was introduced Lenin said:

We are now retreating, going back, as it were; but we are doing this, retreating first, in order to prepare for a longer leap forward. It was only on this condition that we retreated in pursuing our New Economic Policy . . . in order to start a persistent advance after our retreat. (Lenin, *Selected Works,* Vol. IX, p. 376.)

The results of the past year show beyond a doubt that the Party is successfully carrying out this decisive advice of Lenin in the course of its work. . . .

The expansion of the creative initiative and labour enthusiasm of the masses has been stimulated by three main factors: (a) the fight — by means of *self-criticism* — against bureaucracy, which shackles the labour initiative and labour activity of the masses; (b) the fight — by means of *Socialist emulation* — against the labour-shirkers and disrupters of proletarian labour discipline; and finally (c) the fight — by the introduction of the *uninterrupted* week — against routine and inertia in in-

From J. V. Stalin, "A Year of Great Change (On the Occasion of the Twelfth Anniversary of the October Revolution)" and "Problems of Agrarian Policy in the USSR (Speech Delivered at the Conference of Marxist Students of the Agrarian Question, December 27, 1929)," in *Problems of Leninism* (Moscow: Foreign Languages Publishing House, 1940). Pp. 294–298, 302–305, 308–309, 325–326.

dustry. As a result we have a tremendous achievement on the labour front in the form of labour enthusiasm and emulation among the millions of the working class in all parts of our vast country. The significance of this achievement is truly inestimaable, for only the labour enthusiasm and zeal of the millions can guarantee the progressive increase of labour productivity without which the final victory of Socialism over capitalism is inconceivable. . . .

. . . During the past year we have in the main successfully solved the *problem of accumulation* for capital construction in heavy industry; we have *accelerated* the development of the production of means of production and have created the prerequisites for transforming our country into a *metal* country. This is our second fundamental *achievement* during the past year.

The problem of light industry presents no exceptional difficulties. We solved that problem several years ago. The problem of heavy industry is more difficult and more important. It is *more difficult* because it demands colossal investments of capital, and, as the history of industrially backward countries has shown, heavy industry cannot be developed without extensive long-term loans. It is *more important* because, unless we develop heavy industry, we can build no industry whatever, we cannot carry out any industrialization. And as we have never received, nor are we receiving, either long-term loans or credits for any lengthy period, the acuteness of the problem becomes more than obvious. It is precisely for this reason that the capitalists of all countries refuse us loans and credits; they believe that, left to our own resources, we cannot cope with the problem of accumulation, that we are bound to fail in the task of reconstructing our heavy industry, and will at last be compelled to come to them cap in hand and sell ourselves into bondage.

But the results of the past year tell us a different story. The significance of the results of the past year lies in the fact that the calculations of Messieurs the capitalists have been shattered. The past year has shown that in spite of the open and covert financial blockade of the U.S.S.R. we did not sell ourselves into bondage to the capitalists; that, with our own resources, we successfully solved the problem of accumulation and laid the foundation for heavy industry. Even the most inveterate enemies of the working class cannot deny this now. Indeed, since capital investments in large-scale industry last year amounted to over 1,600,000,000 rubles[1] (of which about 1,300,000,000 rubles were invested in heavy industry), and capital investments in large-scale industry this year will amount to over 3,400,000,000 rubles (of which over 2,500,000,000 rubles will be invested in heavy industry); and since the gross output of large-scale industry last year showed an increase of 23 per cent, including a 30 per cent increase in the output of heavy industry, and the increase in the gross output of large-scale industry this year should be 32 per cent, including a 46 per cent increase in the output of heavy industry — is it not obvious that the problem of accumulation for the building up of heavy industry no longer presents insuperable difficulties? How can anyone doubt that in developing our heavy industry, we are advancing at an accelerated pace, exceeding our former speed and leaving behind our "traditional" backwardness?

Is it surprising after this that the estimates of the Five-Year Plan were exceeded during the past year, and that the *optimum* variant of the Five-Year Plan, which the bourgeois scribes regarded as "wild fantasy," and which horrified our Right opportunists (Bukharin's group), has actually turned out to be a *minimum* variant?

"The salvation of Russia," says Lenin, "lies not only in a good harvest on the peasant farms — that is not enough; and not only in the good condition of light industry, which

[1] In 1929 the ruble was officially valued at about $.50 U.S. [Editor's note.]

provides the peasantry with consumers' goods — this, too, is not enough. We also need *heavy* industry. . . . Unless we save heavy industry, unless we restore it, we shall not be able to build up any industry; and without heavy industry we shall be doomed as an independent country. . . . Heavy industry needs state subsidies. If we cannot provide them, then we are doomed as a civilized state — let alone as a Socialist state. (Lenin, *Selected Works,* Vol. X, p. 328.)

These are the blunt terms in which Lenin formulated the problem of accumulation and the task of our Party in building up heavy industry.

The past year has shown that our Party is successfully coping with this task, resolutely overcoming all obstacles in its path.

This does not mean, of course, that industry will not encounter any more serious difficulties. The task of building up heavy industry involves not only the problem of accumulation. It also involves the problem of cadres, the problem (a) of *enlisting* tens of thousands of Soviet-minded technicians and experts for the work of Socialist construction, and (b) of *training* new Red technicians and Red experts from among the working class. While the problem of accumulation may in the main be regarded as solved, the problem of cadres still awaits solution. And the problem of cadres is now — when we are engaged in the technical reconstruction of industry — the decisive problem of Socialist construction. . . .

The assertions of the Right opportunists (Bukharin's group) to the effect (a) that the peasants would not join the collective farms; (b) that the speedy development of collective farming would only arouse mass discontent and drive a wedge between the peasantry and the working class, (c) that the "high-road" of Socialist development in the rural districts is *not* the collective farms, *but* the cooperative societies; and (d) that the development of collective farming and the offensive against the capitalist elements in the rural districts may in the end deprive the country of grain al-

together — all these assertions have also collapsed and crumbled to dust. They have all collapsed and crumbled to dust as old bourgeois-liberal rubbish.

Firstly, the peasants have joined the collective farms; they have joined in whole villages, whole volosts, whole districts.

Secondly, the mass collective-farm movement is not weakening the bond, but, on the contrary, is strengthening it by putting it on a new, production basis. Now even the blind can see that if there is any serious dissatisfaction among the great bulk of the peasantry it is not because of the collective-farm policy of the Soviet government, but because the Soviet government is unable to keep pace with the growth of the collective-farm movement in supplying the peasants with machines and tractors.

Thirdly, the controversy about the "high-road" of Socialist development in the rural districts is a scholastic controversy, worthy of young petty-bourgeois liberals of the type of Eichenwald and Slepkov. It is obvious that, as long as there was no mass collective-farm movement, the "high-road" was the lower forms of the cooperative movement — supply and marketing cooperatives; but when the higher form of the cooperative movement — the collective farm — appeared, the latter became the "high-road" of development. The high-road (without quotation marks) of Socialist development in the rural districts is Lenin's cooperative plan, which embraces all forms of agricultural cooperation, from the lowest (supply and marketing) to the highest (productive collective farms). To *draw a contrast* between collective farming and the cooperative societies is to make a mockery of Leninism and to acknowledge one's own ignorance.

Fourthly, now even the blind can see that without the offensive against the capitalist elements in the rural districts, and without the development of the collective-farm and state-farm movement, we would not have had the decisive successes, achieved this year in the matter of grain collections, nor the tens of millions of

poods of permanent grain reserves which
have already accumulated in the hands of
the state. Moreover, it can now be confidently asserted that, thanks to the growth
of the collective-farm and state-farm movement, we are definitely emerging, or have
already emerged, from the grain crisis.
And if the development of the collective
farms and state farms is accelerated, there
is not the slightest ground for doubt that
in about three years' time our country will
be one of the largest grain countries in
the world, if not *the* largest grain country
in the world.

What is the *new* feature of the present
collective-farm movement? The new and
decisive feature of the present collective-
farm movement is that the peasants are
joining the collective farms not in separate
groups, as was formerly the case, but in
whole villages, whole volosts, whole districts, and even whole areas. And what
does that mean? It means that *the middle
peasant has joined the collective-farm
movement*. This is the basis of that radical
change in the development of agriculture
which represents the most important
achievement of the Soviet government during the past year.

Trotskyism's Menshevik "conception"
that the working class is incapable of leading the great bulk of the peasantry in the
cause of Socialist construction is collapsing
and being smashed to atoms. Now even
the blind can see that the middle peasant
has turned towards the collective farm.
Now it is obvious to all that the Five-Year
Plan of industry and agriculture is a Five-
Year Plan of building a Socialist society,
that those who do not believe in the possibility of building Socialism in our country have no right to greet our Five-Year
Plan.

The last hope of the capitalists of all
countries, who are dreaming of restoring
capitalism in the U.S.S.R. — "the sacred
principle of private property" — is collapsing and vanishing. The peasants, whom
they regarded as material for manuring
the soil for capitalism, are abandoning *en
masse* the lauded banner of "private property" and are taking the path of collectivism, the path of Socialism. The last
hope for the restoration of capitalism is
crumbling. . . .

We are advancing full steam ahead
along the path of industrialization — to
Socialism, leaving behind the age-long
"Russian" backwardness. We are becoming a country of metal, a country of automobiles, a country of tractors. And when
we have put the U.S.S.R. on an automobile, and the muzhik on a tractor, let
the esteemed capitalists, who boast so
loudly of their "civilization," try to over-
take us! We shall see which countries may
then be "classified" as backward and
which as advanced.

. . . Can we advance our socialized industry at an accelerated rate while having
to rely on an agricultural base, such as is
provided by small peasant farming, which
is incapable of expanded reproduction,
and which, in addition, is the predominant
force in our national economy? No, we
cannot. Can the Soviet government and
the work of Socialist construction be, for
any length of time, based on two *different*
foundations: on the foundation of the
most large-scale and concentrated Socialist
industry and on the foundation of the
most scattered and backward, small-com-
modity peasant farming? No, they cannot.
Sooner or later this would be bound to
end in the complete collapse of the whole
national economy. What, then, is the solution? The solution lies in enlarging the
agricultural units, in making agriculture
capable of accumulation, of expanded reproduction, and in thus changing the
agricultural base of our national economy.
But how are the agricultural units to be
enlarged? There are two ways of doing
this. There is the *capitalist* way, which is
to enlarge the agricultural units by introducing capitalism in agriculture — a
way which leads to the impoverishment of
the peasantry and to the development of

capitalist enterprises in agriculture. We reject this way as incompatible with the Soviet economic system. There is a second way: the *Socialist* way, which is to set up collective farms and state farms, the way which leads to the amalgamation of the small peasant farms into large collective farms, technically and scientifically equipped, and to the squeezing out of the capitalist elements from agriculture. We are in favour of this second way.

And so, the question stands as follows: either one way or the other, either *back* — to capitalism or *forward* — to Socialism. There is no third way, nor can there be. The "equilibrium" theory makes an attempt to indicate a third way. And precisely because it is based on a third (nonexistent) way, it is Utopian and anti-Marxian. . . .

Now, as you see, we have the material base which enables us to *substitute* for kulak output the output of the collective farms and state farms. That is why our offensive against the kulaks is now meeting with undeniable success. That is how the offensive against the kulaks must be carried on, if we mean a real offensive and not futile declamations against the kulaks.

That is why we have recently passed from the policy of *restricting* the exploiting proclivities of the kulaks to the policy of *eliminating the kulaks as a class.*

Well, what about the policy of expropriating the kulaks? Can we permit the expropriation of kulaks in the regions of solid collectivization? This question is asked in various quarters. A ridiculous question! We could not permit the expropriation of the kulaks as long as we were pursuing the policy of restricting the exploiting proclivities of the kulaks, as long as we were unable to launch a determined offensive against the kulaks, as long as we were unable to substitute for kulak output the output of the collective farms and state farms. At that time the policy of not permitting the expropriation of the kulaks was necessary and correct. But now? Now the situation is different. Now we are able to carry on a determined offensive against the kulaks, to break their resistance, to eliminate them as a class and substitute for their output the output of the collective farms and state farms. Now, the kulaks are being expropriated by the masses of poor and middle peasants themselves, by the masses who are putting solid collectivization into practice. Now, the expropriation of the kulaks in the regions of solid collectivization is no longer just an administrative measure. Now, the expropriation of the kulaks is an integral part of the formation and development of the collective farms. That is why it is ridiculous and fatuous to expatiate today on the expropriation of the kulaks. You do not lament the loss of the hair of one who has been beheaded.

There is another question which seems no less ridiculous; whether the kulak should be permitted to join the collective farms. Of course not, for he is a sworn enemy of the collective-farm movement. Clear, one would think.

The Fate of the Workers

MANYA GORDON

To a non-Communist Socialist, the First Five Year Plan meant the complete betrayal of the workers' interests for the sake of building new state-owned industry. This is the view argued by Manya Gordon (1882–1945), a native of Russia and at one time a member of the Socialist Revolutionary Party, who came to America and became the wife of the Russian-American editor and author Simeon Strunsky. In her book, *Workers Before and After Lenin*, Miss Gordon undertook to show just how the so-called proletarian revolution had affected the condition of the Russian working class.

THE Communists began by being sincerely loyal to labor, but Lenin soon discovered that the interests of labor were not always the same as the employer's — the state. Tomsky endorsed this stand in the 1920 resolutions. In other words, the Marxist Lenin, acknowledged leader of the Socialist state, and Tomsky, the Marxist trade union leader, agreed that the interests of the workers were not the same as those of the employer in a so-called Socialist state. If that is so, then the state as sole employer can always find a way of prohibiting strikes and other defensive activities of the workers. Any real labor grievance can be declared anti-government. This is precisely the difficulty that Tomsky faced and endeavored to surmount. He did, in fact, accomplish a great deal in the period up to 1928. But ultimately the Communist state as employer had no difficulty in undermining his entire position.

The year 1928, the beginning of the first Five Year Plan, witnessed a complete change in the position of labor. Stalin, Molotov, Kaganovich and others were bent on making of the trade unions an ordinary instrument for the execution of the government plans, completely subservient to the Soviet state. Tomsky and the other trade union leaders opposed this "merging" of the labor organizations with the government because it would turn their representatives into impotent state officials. Stalin and his associates replied to this protest by quoting from the resolutions of the Ninth Congress of which Tomsky was one of the signatories and which declared: "Under the dictatorship of the proletariat the trade unions cease to be organizations which sell labor power to an employing class. There can be no question of trade union opposition to the institutions of the Soviet state. Such opposition is a deviation from Marxism to bourgeois trade unionism." Thus, when convenient the Soviet government declares the trade unions a separate institution concerned only with the interests of the workers, but when necessary the unions become the government.

Tomsky's accusation that Stalin had really adopted Trotzky's doctrine of "merging," so strongly opposed by Lenin, had no effect. The result is history. Tomsky,

Bukharin and Rykov were compelled to resign from the Politbureau and the central committee of the Communist Party, and Stalin packed these powerful agencies with his own followers who did not hesitate to subordinate the interests of labor to the Five Year Plan. In April, 1929, when the subject of the position of the trade unions in the Soviet state was again to the fore Stalin had no difficulty in finding a majority which declared: "In the matter of the trade unions, Bukharin, Rykov, and Tomsky have launched a dangerous trade union opposition to the Party, are actually seeking to weaken the Party's supervision over the trade union movement, and are concealing their 'trade unionistic' tendencies by describing the Party struggle against the shortcomings in the unions as a Trotzkyist shake-up of the unions."

The American reader may consider this a very mild statement in an extremely serious discussion, but in reality it turned out to be a death sentence on these outstanding Communist leaders and on the trade unions. Stalin and his associates declared: "The trade unions are called upon to play a decisive role in the task of building Socialist industry by stimulating labor productivity, labor discipline and Socialist competition, and extirpating all remnants of guild isolation and 'trade unionism.' " Tomsky refused to acquiesce in this method of virtually destroying the trade unions by converting them into agencies of exploitation and was removed from the central committee of the unions. He was succeeded by Shvernik, completely unknown but Stalin's favorite. In order to strengthen Shvernik's authority Stalin made him, in November 1929, a member of the central committee of the Communist Party and there followed the speeding up of the struggle against Tomsky's "bourgeois 'trade unionism' " and the nullification of every trade union prerogative without which the labor organizations became meaningless.

Henceforth the trade unions were compelled to drive the workers, to organize "shock brigades" and "Socialist competition" and bring to trial workers who lagged behind in their quantitative "norms" or in quality. As a result the trade unions in Soviet Russia are to-day a misnomer, and have nothing basically in common with similar organizations in other countries. They are merely a whip over the workers, as plainly shown in the resolutions adopted in the second year of the Five Year Plan, at the Sixteenth Congress of the Communist Party in 1930. The most important part of the declaration reads as follows:

The present phase of Socialist construction raises the problem of the complete reorganization of the activities of the proletarian mass organizations, and among others the trade unions. It is necessary to concentrate on production. The opportunistic ruling group of the old executive of the All Russian Trade Union Central Committee not only showed itself unable to understand the problems of the proletarian dictatorship but opposed the party's reorganization of the work of the trade unions. Displaying "trade unionistic" tendencies, this opportunistic leadership actually carried on a campaign to weaken the party's supervision over the trade union movement. Under the leadership of the party, the trade unions have now removed their bankrupt leaders and have begun a determined fight against the elements of "trade unionism" and opportunism in the trade union movement. To-day the basic factor in energizing and improving the entire work of the trade unions must be Socialist competition and its offspring, the shock brigades. Socialist competition and the shock brigades must become the primary concern of all the constructive activities of the unions. The problem of the trade unions is the organization of Socialist competition and the shock brigades. The trade unions must organize fraternal trials between the best shock brigadiers in order to make the necessary impression on persons who violate labor discipline. The chief concern of all union organizations must be the promotion of outstanding workers to the position of factory directors, officials of departments and their assistants. This reconstruction period demands the participation of the trade unions in the Socialist reconstruction of agriculture. The trade unions must make it their particular business to draw women into production. In approving the dispatch of 25,000 workers for the construction of the kolkhoses [collectivized farms] the Congress declares that the trade unions must make careful preparation and produce new thousands of workers as organizers and directors of kolkhos construction.

The Congress pledges the party organizations and the trade union bodies to increase the propaganda of Leninism in the entire system of the cultural-political work of the unions, to impregnate it with Communist dogma, to remove completely all nonpolitical and narrow cultural elements. The trade unions must fight petty bourgeois leanings and forms of thinking in the labor sphere. The Sixteenth Congress approves the attitude of the new leadership of the trade unions in regard to the absolute support and strengthening of the Profintern [Communist Trade Union International] and trade union amalgamation with the Communist International. The Soviet trade unions must use the Profintern to strengthen their relations with the working class of the Communist and colonial nations for the purpose of waging an unceasing struggle against the reformists in the trade union movement and to promote union with Amsterdam and the strengthening of the revolutionary world trade union movement. The problems which are submitted to the unions can only be solved by a complete reorganization of the work of the trade unions. The basis of the reorganization of the unions is the shock brigade movement.

Here, then, it is bluntly stated that Socialist Competition and its "offspring" the shock brigades must be the primary concern of all constructive work in the unions. Instead of defending the interests of the workers the labor organizations are obliged to disseminate Stalin's brand of Leninism. Actually, it will be recalled, Lenin insisted that the trade unions must be nonpolitical. Stalin now demands that in their Leninist propaganda the unions shall wipe out all nonpolitical elements. This decree was not without a purpose. It was directed against the trade union movement and the solidarity of the workers as well as the Opposition — and it succeeded.

This period of 1929–30 marks the virtual annihilation of the trade unions. Terrorized by threats of execution, by the trials of the nonpartisan engineers in 1930, by the purges of the Mensheviks in 1931, by the expulsion from the trade unions of all of Tomsky's associates and the appointment of Shvernik as head, the trade unions became completely passive. They no longer had the courage to pose any question concerned with the protection of labor. The trade unions were silent when in 1931 it was decreed that a worker could not change his job without the permission of the head of the plant. They were silent when the railroad workers were threatened with years of imprisonment because they had failed to fulfill the prescribed quota in transportation. They were silent when the Soviet [council] of People's Commissars, on February 13, 1931 condemned technically untrained peasant boys to three years' imprisonment because they had unintentionally wrecked some tractors. They were silent on December 4, 1932 when the Soviet of People's Commissars and the central committee of the Communist Party issued the amazing decree putting food supplies and other necessities under the control of the factory directors "in order to strengthen the power of directors of enterprises." In other words, as Pravda saw it, the administrator was given the right to prescribe "the amount of food that should be used."

Beginning with 1930 "the primary purpose of the trade unions," as one secretary of the central committee put it, "was to direct the fight for the completion and over fulfilment by every worker of his prescribed norm of work." The "merging" of the trade unions with the Government was so speedy and complete that wages, sanitation and other labor interests were left in abeyance and the unions concentrated their entire attention on extracting from their members the maximum amount of work. In their anxiety to prove their loyalty to the government the new trade union leaders were more severe than the factory directors. For example, the central committee of the machinists' union called to the attention of the Government, that is the employer, the fact that in several machine works the wage budget was "exceeded," and took steps to turn the matter over to the government prosecutor for bringing criminal charges against the factory directors.

Collective bargaining was relegated to the waste basket. The factory managers became the sole authority on wages and the "amount" of provisions each worker might consume. Without the right to strike or protest in any other way against oppressive measures by the employer the Soviet workers were reduced to the position occupied by labor at the very beginning of Russia's industrialization seventy-five years ago. In fact, Stalin's attitude towards labor was precisely the same as that of the early Russian capitalists towards the erstwhile serfs. The new phraseology and the avowed purpose was different, but that did not make the subjugation of labor any pleasanter.

One might cite as an example the national economic plan of 1931 with two very interesting items. It prescribed for industrial workers an increase in production of 28 per cent, and for that they were to receive a 6 per cent increase in wages. A brief study of these figures will reveal the psychological similarity of government and capitalist as employer. The gross industrial production of 1930 amounted to 25.8 billion rubles. During that year heavy industry employed 4,263,-000 workers. Therefore the gross production per person was 6000 rubles. For the following year the government demanded an increase of 28 per cent, that is, an increase of 1700 rubles. In 1930 the annual average wage of industrial workers was 1035 rubles and the Government was willing to grant a six per cent increase, that is 62 rubles. In other words the Communist Government asked for a 1700 ruble increase in production in return for which it was willing to pay the workers 62 rubles. Actually, instead of an increase there was a reduction in wages. It is an interesting example not only of Communist reasoning about wages but of the method of determining wages. Everything was done by the administration. Labor had not the slightest share in it. . . .

Disorganization of agriculture, the only profitable enterprise in the Soviet Union, was not conducive to higher wages. In fact, the decline in real wages began in 1928. This in turn compelled the official statisticians more energetically to manipulate the wage indexes, but notwithstanding their efforts it became apparent that the industrial worker had to be satisfied with less food. The beginning of farm collectivization in 1929 helped still further to increase the shortage of food in the cities.

The catastrophic state of the country did not, however, prevent the government from writing into the resolutions of the Sixteenth Congress of the Communist Party in July 1930: "During the last five years wages have increased more than 70 per cent, reaching 139 per cent of pre-war real wages." Four months later at a meeting of the Central Executive Committee and the central committee of the Communist Party the utterances were more tempered but not devoid of exaggeration. The resolution declared: "Wages have increased during the first two years of the Five Year Plan (1929–30) by 12 per cent." It did not take the trouble to explain the difference between nominal and real earnings. Actually the rise in nominal wages failed to keep pace with the ever increasing cost of provisions. . . .

In 1928–29 the government statisticians declared: "Because of the shortage of a number of products there took place in the course of the year a curtailment of the consumption of bread, meat and sugar." The following year it was officially acknowledged: "The composition of the workers' dietary has undergone a great change in comparison with the previous year. The decrease in the consumption of breadstuffs was 4.8 per cent, meat 10.1 per cent, sugar 14.2 per cent." Butter, eggs and milk were no longer mentioned. The tightening of the belt continued. In 1930 the shortage became so grave that the government considered it expedient to stop the publication of the food indexes. . . .

As between 1928 and 1930 it is true that the nominal wage of an industrial worker rose from 69 rubles to 83 rubles or 18 per cent; but it has been seen that the cost of food in the same period rose nearly 89 per cent. . . .

. . . The Communist government did not cease to export grain in exchange for its precious machines. Of course, the Czars also exported grain at a time of scarcity, in 1891–93, but their inhumanity was condemned by everybody, including the future Communists. Furthermore, the Czar was not a Marxist. He did not confuse his loyalties. Exporting foodstuffs during a national shortage did not conflict with his class interests. His immediate entourage of landowners, bureaucrats and capitalists did not suffer. Stalin's agrarian policy weighed down on the very people who had a right to expect protection from the Soviet government. The exportation of food while the industrial workers were starving was proof that the Soviet government was more interested in its industrialization formulas than in the proletariat. It revealed a capitalist-employer attitude towards production.

The Plan was the thing, and not the life of the workers. To be sure, it was all done for the good of future generations and in the name of the Socialist state. The exploitation of the Congo by Leopold II, J. D. Rockefeller's early Standard Oil activities and other capitalist aggressions have been defended with the same kind of cant. During the Czarist regime Leo Tolstoy and other great-hearted Russians, with a majority of Russia's "bourgeois

capitalists," came to the aid of the starving masses. The Communists, on the other hand, insisted that the Russian people were not starving while the all-powerful OGPU stifled every protest. Instead of appealing for foreign aid as in 1921–23 when the American people came to the rescue, every effort was made to conceal the catastrophic situation. Foreign correspondents were forbidden to enter the famine stricken areas and the censor deleted all "undesirable" information from their dispatches. "The greater the toll, the more effective the lesson."

But for one very serious qualification the plan to subjugate the peasantry was thus proceeding according to schedule. This exception consisted in the fact that punishment descended not alone upon the officially proclaimed guilty peasant, but upon the innocent industrial worker. To use Lenin's graphic description of the condition of the workers in 1921, more than ten years later in 1931–33, "the enfeeblement of the workers is near the point of complete incapacity for work." Lack of food endangered the execution of the Five Year Plan. Had Lenin been alive he would have very likely taken drastic measures against this suicidal agricultural policy. Joseph Stalin was of sterner metal than the founder of Russian Communism. To be sure, Lenin in his courageous retreat in 1921 — the New Economic Policy — was in some degree motivated by the fact that the Communists were not sufficiently entrenched to risk a showdown. By 1930 thirteen years of Communist rule fortified Stalin's belief in the invincibility of the Soviet state and his personal authority. Power developed in him the capitalist-employer psychology, but an autocrat who sees himself as an industrialist without actually understanding the industrial requirements of the country is a menace.

Collectivization: The Method

MERLE FAINSOD

In 1941 the advancing German army captured most of the Communist Party archive in the city of Smolensk. In 1945 this material fell into the hands of the American army and was microfilmed before being returned to the Russians. Merle Fainsod (1907–   ), Professor of Government and Director of the Russian Research Center at Harvard University, has woven this secret documentary material of the nineteen-twenties and thirties into a unique book on the inner workings of the Soviet government in an individual province. The Smolensk documents show, through official Communist eyes, the uncensored story of the collectivization of the peasants in 1929 and 1930.

THE LIQUIDATION OF THE KULAKS
AS A CLASS

The grain collection campaign of 1929, as it turned out, was merely a prelude to a far more drastic operation, the decision to liquidate the kulak as a class and to lay the groundwork for total collectivization. The signal for the all-out drive was given at the end of 1929, and soon after the turn of the year the operation was launched in various parts of the Western Oblast [Province]. The Smolensk Archive provides a particularly rich record of the execution of the operation in Velikiye Luki okrug [sub-province]; it will be described here in some detail.

On January 28, 1930, the Party committee of Velikiye Luki okrug approved a proposal to deport kulaks from the okrug and to confiscate their property. Two OGPU officials (Kolosov and Dabolin) were designated to prepare a plan of action. On January 30 the Party committee approved the following arrangements: (1) to enlarge the okrug OGPU apparatus by four more members and to mobilize an additional eleven people from the OGPU reserve; (2) to make 10,000 rubles available to the OGPU to finance the added

personnel; (3) to release okrug militia forces from other duties and to use them in the dekulakization campaign; (4) to supply arms from the "mobilization reserves" to all participants; and (5) to postpone putting into effect an earlier okrug decision to take down all church bells and close churches in order not to arouse general peasant resistance.

March 1, 1930, was set as a target date for the completion of the operation. On February 6 special okrug and raion [district] troikas were designated to direct activities. In each case the troika consisted of the first secretary of the Party committee, the chairman of the soviet executive committee (ispolkom) and the head of the OGPU. The okrug Party committee also arranged to dispatch twenty-six people to the raions to assist the local authorities.

On February 12, a top-secret letter was sent to all raitroikas [district troikas] outlining detailed instructions for the conduct of the operation. Working through the raikoms [district party committees] and the village soviets, the raitroikas were to undertake a prompt inventory of all kulak property, meanwhile warning the kulaks that if they were caught in the unauthorized sale of any of their property, all of it would immediately be confiscated. The inventory was to be completed within a two-week period.

The letter ordered the raitroikas to divide all kulak households into three groups, according to the degree of danger which they presented to the soviet authorities and the severity of the punishment which was to be imposed on them. The first and most dangerous group, described as "the counterrevolutionary kulak aktiv [active group]," was to be arrested by the OGPU. The raitroikas were authorized to make additions to this "list" on the basis of recommendations emerging from meetings of poor peasants and agricultural laborers. Incriminating material was to be forwarded to the OGPU. The second category consisted of "certain (separate) elements of the kulak aktiv," especially from among the richest peasants and "quasi-landowners," who were to be deported to "far-off" parts of the Soviet Union. The remaining kulaks were to be removed from areas scheduled for "total collectivization," but were not to be deported from the okrug. For such kulaks the raion executive committees were to provide special land parcels carved out of "eroded" areas, "swamp-lands in woods," and other soil "in need of improvement."

Families of Group I and II kulaks were to be deported from the okrug on the approval of the okrug troika. Property of Group I households was to be confiscated immediately and handed over to neighboring collective farms either in existence or in process of organization. In the absence of such farms, the property was to be delivered to the nearest functioning kolkhoz [collective farm]. Property of Group II households was to be confiscated gradually, with confiscation timed to coincide with deportation schedules. In order to "guide" the raions in conducting the operation, the okrug troika supplied each raion with an "orientation number" of Group I kulaks who were to be arrested

and Group II kulaks who were to be deported. . . .

Protocols of the okrug troika mirror the confusion and disorganization of the period. Despite apparently precise directives and instructions, many raion and village authorities went their own way, interpreting the kulak category broadly to embrace middle and even poor peasants who were opposed to collectivization, evicting kulak families with Red Army connections, and rarely bothering to supply the okrug troika with supporting data to justify their decisions. In the first flush of the dekulakization campaign, "excesses" were commonplace. An OGPU report of February 28, 1930, provides a matter-of-fact recital of some of the antics of the dekulakizers. According to the report, in many villages "certain members of the workers' brigades and officials of lower echelons of the Party-soviet apparatus" deprived members of kulak and middle peasant households of their clothing and warm underwear (directly from the body), "confiscated" head-wear from children's heads, and removed shoes from people's feet. The perpetrators divided the "confiscated" goods among themselves; the food they found was eaten on the spot; the alcohol they uncovered was consumed immediately, resulting in drunken orgies. In one case a worker tore a warm blouse off a woman's back, put it on himself with the words, "You wore it long enough, now I will wear it." The slogan of many of the dekulakization brigades was: "drink, eat — it's all ours." One commune, in search of more and richer "confiscations," commenced to dekulakize kulaks of the bordering village soviet. As the kulaks in question were administratively under the "jurisdiction" of another kolkhoz, a struggle ensued between the communards and the kolkhozniks. The communards under the direction of their Party secretary absconded with much of the money and property of the kulaks before the kolkhoz could act. In the process, even eyeglasses were torn from the peasants' faces; kasha [porridge] was "confiscated" straight from the oven and either eaten or used to smear the ikons. When the OGPU investigated the whereabouts of the "confiscated" property, the commune destroyed the original inventory lists and wrote new ones.

Another OGPU report, dated February 23, 1930, noted that middle and even poor peasants were being arrested by "anybody" — by raion emissaries, village soviet members, kolkhoz chairmen, and any one in any way connected with collectivization. People were being transported to militia prisons without the slightest grounds or evidence. Although the raion authorities were aware of this, they were reluctant to interfere so as "not to undermine the authority of the village soviet" responsible for the arrest. Some poor peasants and "activists" were blackmailing the richer peasants, taking bribes for removing them from the confiscation or deportation lists. In many cases, confiscated cattle was not being fed and was starving to death.

Still another report pointed out that the looting in the villages had induced an atmosphere of panic among the well-to-do peasants. According to this report, a wave of suicides was sweeping the richer households; kulaks were killing their wives and children and then taking their own lives. In order to prevent complete property confiscation, many kulaks and their wives were entering into fictitious divorces, in the hope that at least some property and the lives of wives and children would be spared. Sensing their impending doom, kulaks in growing numbers were fleeing to the east (Moscow, the Urals, Siberia). They dekulakized themselves by selling out all they owned, or leaving their property with relatives and friends, or simply abandoning their fields and homes.

Occasionally kulaks also found friends and protectors at court. Chairmen of village soviets were reported as befriending kulaks by exempting valuable kulak property from confiscation; some Party members defended kulaks because of their previous humanitarian behavior toward poor peasants. Many poor and middle peasants considered dekulakization unjust and harmful, refused to vote approval of deportation and expropriation measures, hid kulak property, and warned their kulak friends of pending searches and requisitions. In many cases poor and middle peasants were reported as collecting signatures to petitions testifying to the loyalty and good character of kulaks, millers, and other well-to-do elements. The high-handed tactics of indiscriminate and arbitrary confiscation and deportation turned many poor and middle peasants into bitter opponents of the regime.

At this point the Party leadership decided to call a halt to the "excesses" it had set in motion. On February 20, 1930, Rumyantsev[1] addressed a letter to all okrug Party secretaries, calling attention to the fact that, despite "exhaustive and precise instructions" from the obkom [provincial party committee], deviations in dekulakization policy were continuing. Among these he particularly condemned: (1) the dekulakization of middle peasants and the "mass-inclusion" of such peasants in kulak lists based only on "vicious rumor" and "possible provocation"; (2) the lawless actions of dekulakization brigades which "interfere with normal administrative processes"; (3) the use of Red Army units in carrying out dekulakization; (4) the spreading of the slogans of dekulakization (with the same inadmissible methods) to the city Nepmen; (5) the actions of drunken soldiers and Komsomols [young Communists] who "without mass preparation" were "arbitrarily closing village churches, breaking ikons, and threatening the peasants."

The Rumyantsev letter was followed by a top-secret obkom circular of March 2 reprimanding the okrug Party commit-

[1] Ivan P. Rumyantsev, First Secretary of the Communist Party for the Smolensk Province, until he was purged in 1937. [Editor's note.]

tees for "brutal" abuses committed by raion and village officials against the "dekulakized." Brought up short by these warnings and Stalin's "Dizziness from Success" article (published in *Pravda* on March 2), the okrug troikas initiated a review of all raion decisions on dekulakization. In a typical action in Velikiye Luki okrug involving a list of 121 dekulakized households in Siebezhsky raion, the raitroika's decisions were rejected in forty-four cases, and eight cases were referred to the OGPU for further investigation. The OGPU quickly adjusted to the new line and followed the lead of the okrug troikas in overruling raion decisions. The raitroikas were instructed to return confiscated property to those peasants who had been "unjustly" dekulakized. Like other posthumous efforts to render justice, the instructions proved easier to issue than to execute.

KULAK DEPORTATIONS

Meanwhile, kulak deportations gathered momentum. The most detailed description of the deportations in the Smolensk Archive are to be found in OGPU reports of March 1931 [2] dealing with the situation in the Roslavl area. In the rural district of Roslavl preparations for deportation began on February 15, 1931.[2] Lists of all kulaks and well-to-do peasants were collected from the village soviets. But these lists, the OGPU emissary complained, "failed to provide the information necessary to do the impending job." Consequently, personal questionnaires were circulated to 215 potential victims under the guise of checking the correctness of their tax liabilities. On March 18, the raitroika reviewed the questionnaires and condemned seventy-four households to liquidation. On the evening of March 19, the raitroika assembled its emissaries at a central point, gave them instructions, and assigned two households to each emissary. The operation was to

[2] Evidently a misprint which should read "1930." [Editor's note.]

be completed that same night. But "not all went smoothly." In a number of cases the emissaries stalled, conducted drawn-out meetings with poor peasants, and in general "failed to arrange the job in a tightly conspiratorial fashion." As a result kulaks were forewarned, and the emissaries failed to find those marked for deportation. Some emissaries allowed "tearful goodbyes to be drawn out" during which many able-bodied men slipped away. A number of kulaks succeeded in smuggling their property to poorer relatives. All in all, thirty-two families were deported from the raion; the rest fled, and the OGPU head stated that measures were being taken to find them. He complained that many emissaries had made "grave mistakes"; the wife of one emissary, a Komsomol, publicly expressed grief and sympathy for the deported. "We are no longer people," she was quoted as having said; "we are animals." But most Komsomols were lauded for having done an outstanding job, "better than that of responsible officials." According to the report, poor peasants were "generally pleased" with the progress of events. But middle peasants were "confused and unnerved." "Our turn will come soon," they kept repeating. . . .

PROBLEMS OF KOLKHOZ ORGANIZATION

Prior to the application of this pressure, the kolkhoz movement was slow to take root in the Western Oblast. Indeed, the First Five Year Plan for the oblast contemplated that only 8.6 per cent of the peasant households would be enrolled in kolkhozes by 1932–33. On October 1, 1928, the actual percentage of collectivization was an almost infinitesimal 0.8 per cent. By October 1, 1929, it had increased to only 2.5 per cent. From that point on, in accordance with directions from the center to liquidate the kulak and intensify the organization of kolkhozes, the tempo of collectivization mounted swiftly. On March 1, 1930, the Western Oblast reported that 38.8 per cent of all hired-labor, poor-peasant, and middle-peasant households were collectivized.

What happened in the intervening five months is perhaps best portrayed in the language of the peasants themselves. The Smolensk Archive contains a collection of peasants' letters (most of them unpublished) written during this period to the editors of the oblast peasant newspaper, *Nasha Derevnya* (Our Village). They vividly convey what was happening in the countryside and how the letter writers felt about it. "Dear Comrades," wrote Ivan Trofimovich Chuyunkov from the village of Yushkovo:

For a long time I have wanted to write you about what you have written on collectivization in your newspaper *Nasha Derevnya*.

In the first place I will give you my address so that you will not suspect that I am a kulak or one of his parasites. I am a poor peasant. I have one hut, one barn, one horse, 3 dessyatins of land, and a wife and three children. Dear Comrades, as a subscriber to your newspaper . . . I found in No. 13/85 for February 15 a letter from a peasant who writes about the life of kolkhoz construction. I, a poor peasant, reading this letter, fully agreed with it. This peasant described life in the kolkhoz completely correctly. Isn't it true that all the poor peasants and middle peasants do not want to go into the kolkhoz at all, but that you drive them in by force? For example, I'll take my village soviet of Yushkovo. A brigade of soldiers came to us. This brigade went into all the occupied homes, and do you think that they organized a kolkhoz? No, they did not organize it. The hired laborers and the poor peasants came out against it and said they did not want *corvée*, they did not want serfdom . . . I'll write more of my village soviet. When the Red Army brigade left, they sent us a kolkhoz organizer from Bryansk okrug. And whom do you think this Comrade signed up? Not poor peasants, not hired laborers, but kulaks, who, sensing their own ruin, enter the kolkhoz. And your organizer . . . takes to evil deeds. At night, together with the Komsomolites, he takes everything away from the peasants, both surpluses and taxes, which you fleece from the peasants. Of course agricultural taxes are necessary, self-taxation is necessary, fire taxes are necessary, tractoriza-

tion is necessary. But where can the toiling peasant get this money if not from the seeds of his products? And these Party people stay up all night and rob the peasants. If he brings a pud, if he brings 5, it's all the same. I would propose that you let the peasant live in greater freedom than he does now, and then we won't beg you to get rid of such a gang, for we ourselves will eliminate them.

Wrote one Pyotr Gorky:

In the first place, I, a citizen of the village of Muzhyno . . . tell you, our government and also the editors, that we toiling peasants, poor peasants, and also the middle peasants see that life is bad, but nevertheless we have endured it. But when we got to the year 1930, we saw that we were ruined. We have bad land and little of it in the village of Muzhyno, and we had grain and potato requisitions, and they took them from us by force, both from the poor peasants and from the middle peasants. Simply speaking, it was robbery . . . We ourselves do not know what to do. Every day they send us lecturers asking us to sign up for such-and-such a kolkhoz for eternal slavery, but we don't want to leave our good homes. It may be a poor little hut, but it's mine, a poor horse, but it's mine. Among us, he who works more has something to eat. We peasants are used to working, but you, our government, change the pay every day arbitrarily . . . We ourselves don't know what to do. There aren't any nails, there is nothing and life is bad. We will not be able to eat in the kolkhoz . . . Therefore we beg you to turn the rudder of the kolkhoz movement and let the peasant own property. Then we assure you that everyone will be able to put more surpluses on the market, and trade will be free. We poor peasants ask you to change everything, to give us freedom, and then we will be glad to help the state.

Wrote still another peasant:

Comrades, you write that all the middle peasants and poor peasants join the kolkhoz voluntarily, but it is not true. For example, in our village of Podbuzhye, all do not enter the kolkhoz willingly. When the register made the rounds, only 25% signed it, while 75% did not. They collected seeds by frightening [the peasants] with protocols and arrests. If any one spoke against it, he was threatened with arrest and forced labor. You are deceived in this, Comrades. Collective life can be created when the entire mass of the peasants goes voluntarily, and not by force . . . I beg you not to divulge my name, because the Party people will be angry. [Signed] POLZIKOV.

Another peasant wrote:

They [the kolkhoz organizers] use force and threats against those who do not enter the kolkhoz — they take away their land and deport them out of the bounds of the village. I ask you . . . whether they can behave like that and take away the land and deport an invalid poor peasant like me?

The following letter is in a similar vein:

Comrade editor . . . If, as you write, they [the peasants] join the kolkhozes voluntarily, why do you send brigades who send you to prison for the slightest resistance against the kolkhoz? Did the people think that they would live this way after they received freedom? Now it happens that freedom is not a word, but prison is a word. Say something against collectivization, and you're put in prison . . . If you took a vote, you would only find half of a per cent who joined the kolkhoz voluntarily. Each one thinks it is a terrible thing; each one wants to be a master and not a slave . . .

The same hatred of the kolkhoz was expressed by Ivan Bogdanov from the village of Lodosh:

My household consists of one horse, 3 sheep, 4 dessyatins of land for 7 consumers . . . I ask you to answer the question whether it is compulsory to enter the kolkhoz. I think not, but they gave us complete collectivization in Usvyatsk raion. I am sure that if you came and took a vote that not more than 15% would be in favor of the kolkhoz. All the people destroy their livestock, saying, "It doesn't matter, you have to go into the kolkhoz against your will" . . . Do not force the people to join the kolkhoz — there isn't any sense to it . . . It's better to hang yourself than to join the kolkhoz; it's better not to be born than to join the kolkhoz . . .

These extracts, which are culled largely from the letters of poor peasants, underline the role that force played in accel-

erating the tempo of collectivization. Nor was the opposition to collectivization confined to verbal protests. In some instances, at least, violence was met with violence, and the reports of the procurator [prosecutor] and the OGPU for this period are replete with examples. On September 30, 1929, Lebedev, the oblast procurator, reported the following incident to the obkom: "On September 2, of this year, in the village of Lyalichi, Klintsy okrug, a mob of 200 people made an open attack on the kolkhozniks who were going out to work the fields. This attack consisted of the dispersal of the kolkhozniks from the field, the destruction of their equipment, clothes, etc. They chased after the leaders of the kolkhoz, but the latter succeeded in saving themselves by fleeing. The majority of the attackers were women, who were armed with staves, pitchforks, spades, axes, etc. On the night of September 3 a threshing floor with all the harvest, belonging to a member of the kolkhoz, was destroyed by fire." Thirty-nine persons were brought to trial for their participation in this affair. According to a special Information Bulletin of the Procurator of the Western Oblast for July-October 1929, "The most widespread means of struggle against kolkhoz construction (after its organization) is arson." Numerous instances are cited where barns, haystacks, and houses belonging to kolkhozes were burned. Also listed as "very typical" are "cases of mass outbursts against the kolkhozes, primarily by women, under the leadership of kulaks and wealthy people." One such incident in the village of Golshino where a kolkhoz was being organized is described as follows:

The local priest came out as an ardent oppositionist, carrying on open agitation among the women to resist the organization of the kolkhoz. On . . . the day designated for the division of land under the future kolkhoz, a crowd of women went to the fields, armed with axes, staves, and pitchforks, to beat the kolkhozniks. Meeting the surveyor and the secretary of the village soviet on the way, they began to insult them, tried to break the surveyor's instruments, and beat the secretary. Then they went on to the field and pulled out all the posts which bounded the kolkhoz. In the investigation of this case it was found that not enough mass work had been done by the local Party organs while the kolkhoz was being organized. The local priest occupied himself with "agitation work" . . . coming out openly against the closing of the church, and he went around to the peasants in their yards and summoned the women to demonstrate against the kolkhoz. Nobody from the volost Party and soviet organs knew about the agitation, for the organization of the kolkhoz had been entrusted to the surveyor . . ."

The story of the first great collectivization drive (1929–30) as it unfolds in the Smolensk Archive is a record of "storm" tactics and stubborn peasant opposition, of grandiose projects and "paper" victories. The regime in many cases could not trust its local soviet functionaries to carry the brunt of the drive, and as a result workers were mobilized from the factories to organize the kolkhozes. The "25,000'ers," as they were called, did not find their task easy. Here is a letter which a group of them wrote to their responsible superior, one Comrade Stolbov:

We workers have been sent to the Western Oblast, Voskresensk raion, Vyazma okrug, to work in the kolkhozes. But our living conditions do not permit us to work as we should.

They have placed us in kolkhozes which have only been established a month or less. They sent us into leading work in kolkhozes where there were supposed to be funds, and they told us we would be paid out of the funds of the kolkhoz, but it didn't happen that way at all. They put most of us 16 people in such conditions in Voskresensk raion that we beg for help. They put us in kolkhozes with economies where there are no funds, where property has not yet been socialized, and we workers must be the organizers of the kolkhozes. Those of us who have arrived in the small kolkhozes are not given either money or food; they receive us worse than beggars. There are no living quarters . . .

In view of all these conditions, the work is not progressing; we live and do not know what the future will bring, how and what we will eat. What they told us when they sent us to work in the country is not at all so; they said that we would work in kolkhozes and would receive up to 30–40 rubles per month, but we didn't even receive 5 rubles a month, and there is not even food, and we don't eat.

The local organizations take a miserable attitude toward this and do not know themselves how we will eat and do not do anything about it.

Under such conditions of life as we have described above, it is impossible to work, and there is only one way out. To work longer is impossible, and to live in such circumstances is impossible; we must flee home, and then see what will happen. We ask the okrug committee of the Party to answer this and to tell us what to do.

Economics and Personality

ALEC NOVE

The complex issues of economics underlying Stalin's Five-Year Plans and the collectivization of the peasants have been succinctly evaluated by the British economist Alec Nove (1915–   ), a leading authority on the Soviet economic system. Nove surveys the problem in the political and psychological respects as well as the strictly economic, in an effort to judge what personal choices or political requirements caused Stalinism to become an economically unavoidable outcome.

STALIN has suffered a dramatic post-mortem demotion, and a monument to his victims is to be erected in Moscow. The present Soviet leadership is thus disassociating itself publicly from many of the highly disagreeable features of Stalin's rule, while claiming for the Party and the Soviet system the credit for making Russia a great economic and military power. Is this a logically consistent standpoint? How far was Stalin, or Stalinism, an integral, unavoidable, "necessary" part of the achievement of the period? How much of the evil associated with the Stalin system is attributable to the peculiar character of the late dictator, and how much was the consequence of the policies adopted by the large majority of the Bolshevik party, or of the effort of a small and dedicated minority to impose very rapid industrialisation on a peasant country? . . .

. . . The idea of "necessity" does not of course mean that the leader had to be a Georgian with a long moustache, but rather a tough dictator ruling a totalitarian state of the Stalinist type. What were the practical alternatives before the Bolsheviks in the late 'twenties, which contributed to the creation of the Stalinist régime, or, if one prefers a different formulation, gave the opportunity to ambitious men to achieve so high a degree of absolutism?

The key problem before the Bolsheviks concerned the linked questions of industrialisation and political power. They felt they had to industrialise for several reasons, some of which they shared with non-Bolshevik predecessors. Thus the Tsarist minister, Count Witte, as well as Stalin, believed that to achieve national strength and maintain independence, Russia needed a modern industry, especially heavy industry. The national-defence argument, re-labelled "defense of the revolution," was greatly strengthened by the belief that the Russian revolution was in constant danger from a hostile capitalist environment, militarily and technically far stronger than the U.S.S.R. Then there was the belief that the building of socialism or communism involved industrialisation, and, more immediately, that a "proletarian dictatorship" was insecure so long as it ruled in an overwhelmingly petty-bourgeois, peasant, environment. There had to be a large increase in the number and importance of the proletariat, while the rise of a rich "kulak" class in the vil-

From Alec Nove, "Was Stalin Really Necessary?" *Encounter*, April 1962, pp. 86–92. Reprinted by permission of the editors.

lages was regarded as a dangerous (or potentially dangerous) resurgence of capitalism. It was clear, by 1927, that it was useless to wait for "world revolution" to solve these problems. These propositions were common to the protagonists of the various platforms of the middle 'twenties. Thus even the "moderate" Bukharin wrote: "If there were a fall in the relative weight of the working class in its political and its social and class power, . . . this would subvert the basis of the proletarian dictatorship, the basis of our government." He too spoke in principle of the "struggle against the kulak, against the capitalist road," and warned of the "kulak danger." He too, even in the context of an attack on Zinoviev and the "left" opposition, argued the need for "changing the production relations of our country."

Until about 1927, a rapid rise in industrial production resulted from (or, "was a result of") the reactivation of pre-revolutionary productive capacity, which fell into disuse and disrepair in the civil war period. However, it now became urgent to find material and financial means to expand the industrial base. This at once brought the peasant problem to the fore. The revolution had distributed land to 25 million families, most of whom were able or willing to provide only small marketable surpluses. Supplies of food to the towns and for export fell, peasant consumption rose. Yet the off-farm surplus must grow rapidly to sustain industrialisation, especially where large-scale loans from abroad could scarcely be expected. As the "left" opposition vigorously pointed out, the peasant, the bulk of the population, had somehow to be made to contribute produce and money, to provide the bulk of "primitive Socialist accumulation."

The arguments around these problems were inextricably entangled in the political factional struggles of the 'twenties. The moderate wing, led by Bukharin, believed that it was possible to advance slowly towards industrialisation "at the pace of a tortoise," a pace severely limited by what the peasant was willing to do voluntarily. This was sometimes described as "riding towards socialism on a peasant nag." The logic of this policy demanded priority for developing consumers' goods industries, to make more cloth to encourage the peasants to sell more food. At first, Stalin sided with the moderates.

The case against the Bukharin line was of several different kinds. Firstly, free trade with the peasants could only provide adequate surpluses if the better-off peasants (*i.e.*, those known as *kulaks*) were allowed to expand, since they were the most efficient producers and provided a large part of the marketable produce. Yet all the Bolshevik leaders (including, despite momentary aberrations, Bukharin himself) found this ideologically and politically unacceptable. A strong group of independent, rich peasants was Stolypin's dream as a basis for Tsardom. It was the Bolshevik's nightmare, as totally inconsistent in the long run with their rule or with a socialist transformation of "petty-bourgeois" Russia. But this made the Bukharin approach of doubtful internal consistency. This was understood at the time by intelligent non-party men. Thus the famous economist Kondratiev, later to perish in the purges, declared in 1927: "If you want a higher rate of accumulation . . . then the stronger elements of the village must be allowed to exploit (the weaker)," in other words that the "kulaks" must expand their holdings and employ landless labourers. The "peasant nag" could not pull the cart; or it, and the peasant, would pull in the wrong direction.

A second reason concerned the pace of the tortoise. The Bolsheviks were in a hurry. They saw themselves threatened by "imperialist interventionists." Even though some war scares were manufactured for factional reasons, the Party as a whole believed that war against them would come before very long. This argued not merely for speed, but also for priority to *heavy* and not light industry, since it provided a basis for an arms industry.

Still another reason was a less tangible but still very real one: the necessity of maintaining political *élan*, of not appearing to accept for an indefinite period a policy of gradualism based on the peasant, which would have demoralised the Party and so gravely weakened the régime. It was widely felt, in and out of Russia, that by 1927 the régime had reached a *cul-de-sac*. I have in front of me a contemporary Menshevik pamphlet published abroad, by P. A. Garvi, which describes its dilemma quite clearly, and indeed the political and economic problem was extremely pressing: to justify its existence, to justify the Party dictatorship in the name of the proletariat, a rapid move forward was urgent; but such a move forward would hardly be consistent with the "alliance with the peasants" which was the foundation of the policy of the moderates in the 'twenties. Stalin at this point swung over towards the left, and his policy of all-out industrialisation and collectivisation was a means of breaking out of the *cul-de-sac*, of mobilising the Party to smash peasant resistance, to make possible the acquisition of farm surpluses without having to pay the price which any free peasants or free peasant associations would have demanded. He may well have felt he had little choice. It is worth quoting from the reminiscences of another Menshevik [N. Valentinov], who in the late 'twenties was working in the Soviet planning organs: "The financial base of the first five-year plan, *until Stalin found it in levying tribute on the peasants, in primitive accumulation by the methods of Tamerlane*, was extremely precarious. . . . (It seemed likely that) everything would go to the devil. . . . No wonder that no one, literally no one, of the well-informed economists, believed or could believe in the fulfillment (of the plan)."

It does not matter in the present context whether Stalin made this shift through personal conviction of its necessity, or because this seemed to him to be a clever power-manœuvre. The cleverness in any case largely consisted in knowing that he would thus strengthen his position by becoming the spokesman of the view which was widely popular among Party activists. The "leftists," destroyed organisationally by Stalin in earlier years, had a considerable following. Stalin's left-turn brought many of them to his support — though this did not save them from being shot in due course on Stalin's orders. It is probably the case that he had at this time genuine majority support within the Party for his policy, though many had reservations about certain excesses, of which more will be said. But if this be so, the policy as such cannot be attributed to Stalin personally, and therefore the consequences which flowed from its adoption must be a matter of more than personal responsibility.

Let us examine some of these consequences. Collectivisation could not be voluntary. Rapid industrialisation, especially with priority for heavy industry, meant a reduction in living standards, despite contrary promises in the first five-year plans. This meant a sharp increase in the degree of coercion, in the powers of the police, in the unpopularity of the régime. The aims of the bulk of the people were bound to be in conflict with the aims of the Party. It should be added that this conflict is probably bound to arise in some form wherever *the state* is responsible for financing rapid industrialisation; the sacrifices are then imposed by political authority, and the masses of "small" people do not and cannot provide voluntarily the necessary savings, since in the nature of things their present abstinence cannot be linked with a future return which they as individuals can identify. However, this possibly unavoidable unpopularity was greatly increased in the U.S.S.R. by the sheer pace of the advance and by the attack on peasant property, and, as we shall see, both these factors reacted adversely on production of consumers' goods and so led to still further hardships and even greater unpopularity. The strains and priorities involved in a rapid move forward required a high degree of economic centralisation, to prevent resources from being diverted to satisfy needs which were urgent but of a non-priority character. In this situation, the Party was the one body capable of carrying out enormous changes and resisting social and economic pressures in a hostile environment; this was bound to affect its structure. For a number of years it had already been in process of transformation from a political into a power machine. The problems involved in the "revolution from above" intensified the process of turning it into an obedient instrument for changing, suppressing, controlling.

This, in turn, required hierarchical subordination, in suppression of discussion; therefore there had to be an unquestioned commander-in-chief. Below him, toughness in executing unpopular orders became the highest qualification for Party office. The emergence of Stalin, and of Stalin-type bullying officials of the sergeant-major species, was accompanied by the decline in the importance of the cosmopolitan journalist-intellectual type of party leader who had played so prominent a role earlier.

The rise of Stalin to supreme authority was surely connected with the belief among many Party members that he was the kind of man who could cope with this kind of situation. Of course, it could well be that Stalin tended to adopt policies which caused him and his type to be regarded as indispensable, and he promoted men to office in the Party because they were loyal to him. Personal ambition, a desire for power, were important factors in shaping events. But this is so obvious, so clearly visible on the surface, that the underlying problems, policy choices and logical consequences of policies need to be stressed.

Let us recapitulate: the Communists needed dictatorial power if they were to continue to rule; if they were to take effective steps towards industrialisation these steps were bound to give rise to problems which would require further tightening of political and economic control. While we cannot say, without much further research, whether a Bukharinite or other moderate policy was impossible, once the decision to move fast was taken this had very radical consequences; the need for a tough, coercive government correspondingly increased. Given the nature of the Party apparatus, the mental and political development of the Russian masses, the logic of police rule, these policies were bound to lead to a conflict with the peasantry and to excesses of various kinds. Thus, given the premises, certain elements of what may be called Stalinism followed, were objective "necessities." In this sense, and to this extent, Stalin was, so to speak, operating within the logical consequences of Leninism.

It is an essential part of Lenin's views that the Party was to seize power and use it to change Russian society; this is what distinguished him from the Mensheviks who believed that conditions for socialism should ripen within society. Lenin also suppressed opposition parties and required stern discipline from his own followers. (It is impossible to ban free speech outside the Party without purging the Party of those who express "wrong" views within it.) Indeed Lenin promoted Stalin because he knew he was tough, would "prepare peppery dishes," though he had last-minute regrets about it. While it would be going too far to describe Stalin as a true Leninist, if only because Lenin was neither personally brutal nor an oriental despot, Stalin undoubtedly carried through some of the logical consequences of Lenin's policies and ideas. This remains true even though Lenin thought that the peasant problem could be solved by voluntary inspiration, and would probably have recoiled at the conditions of forced collectivisation.

Is it necessary to stress that this does not make these actions right, or good? Yes, it is, because so many critics assume that to explain is to justify. So it must be said several times that no moral conclusions follow, that even the most vicious acts by politicians and others generally have causes which must be analysed. We are here only concerned to disentangle the special contribution of Stalin, the extent to which Stalinism was, so to speak, situation-determined. This is relevant, indeed, to one's picture of Stalin's personal responsibility, but in no way absolves him of such responsibility. If in order to do A it proves necessary to do B, we can, after all, refuse to do B, abandon or modify the aim of attaining A, or resign, or, in extreme circumstances — like Stalin's old comrade Ordzhonikidze — commit suicide.

But Stalin's personal responsibility goes far beyond his being the voice and leader of a party majority in a given historical situation. For one cannot possibly argue that all the immense evils of the Stalin era flowed inescapably from the policy decisions of 1928–29. In assessing Stalin's personal role in bringing these evils about, it is useful to approach the facts from two angles. There was, first, the category of evils which sprang from policy choices which Stalin made and which he need not have made; in other words we are here concerned with consequences (perhaps necessary) of unnecessary decisions. The other category consists of evil actions which can reasonably be attributed to Stalin and which are his direct responsibility.

Of course, these categories shade into one another, as do murder and manslaughter. In the first case, the evils were in a sense situation-determined, but Stalin had a large hand in determining the situation. In the second, his guilt is as clear as a politician's guilt can be.

The most obvious examples of the first category are: the brutality of collectivisation and the madly excessive pace of industrial development. In each case, we are dealing with "excessive excesses," since we have already noted that collectivisation

without coercion was impossible, and rapid industrialisation was bound to cause stresses and strains.

Take collectivisation first. Some over-zealous officials were presumably bound to overdo things, especially since the typical Party man was a townsman with no understanding or sympathy for peasants and their problems. But these officials received orders to impose rapid collectivisation, to deport *kulaks*, to seize all livestock, and Stalin was surely the source of these orders. The deportation of the *kulaks* (which in reality meant anyone who voiced opposition to collectivisation) removed at one blow the most efficient farmers. There had been no serious preparation of the measures, no clear orders about how a collective farm should be run. Chinese experience, at least before the communes, suggests that milder ways of proceeding are possible. In any event, the attempt to collectivise all private livestock ended in disaster and a retreat. It is worth reproducing the figures from the official handbook of agricultural statistics:

LIVESTOCK POPULATION
(MILLION OF HEAD)

	1928	1934
Horses	32.1	15.4
Cattle	60.1	33.5
Pigs	22.0	11.5
Sheep	97.3	32.9

Yet already by 1934 private livestock holdings were again permitted, and in 1938 over three-quarters of all cows, over two-thirds of all pigs, nearly two-thirds of all sheep, were in private hands. This is evidence of a disastrous error.

Its consequences were profound. Peasant hostility and bitterness were greatly intensified. For many years there were in fact no net investments in agriculture, since the new tractors merely went to replace some of the slaughtered horses. Acute food shortage made itself felt — though the state's control over produce ensured that most of those who died in the resulting famine were peasants and not townsmen. But once all this happened, the case for coercion was greatly strengthened, the need for police measures became more urgent than ever, the power of the censorship was increased, freedom of speech had still further to be curtailed, as part of the necessities of remaining in power and continuing the industrial revolution in an environment grown more hostile as a result of such policies. So Stalin's policy decisions led to events which contributed greatly to the further growth of totalitarianism and the police state.

The same is true of the attempt to do the impossible on the industrial front in the years of the first five-year plan. Much of the effort was simply wasted, as when food was taken from hungry peasants and exported to pay for machines which rusted in the open or were wrecked by untrained workmen. At the same time, the closing of many private workshops deprived the people of consumers' goods which the state, intent on building steelworks and machine-shops, was quite unable to provide. Again, living standards suffered, the hatred of many citizens for the régime increased, the N.K.V.D. had to be expanded and the logic of police rule followed. But Stalin had a big role in the initial decisions to jump too far too fast. (It is interesting to note that Mao, who should have learnt the lessons of history, repeated many of these mistakes in China's "great leap forward" of 1958–59, which suggests that *there are certain errors which Communists repeatedly commit,* possibly due to the suppression, in "anti-rightist" campaigns, of the voices of moderation and common sense.)

One of the consequences of these acute hardships was isolation from foreign countries. Economists often speak of the "demonstration effect," *i.e.,* of the effect of the knowledge of higher living standards abroad on the citizens of poor and underdeveloped countries. This knowledge may act as a spur to effort — but it also generates resistance to sacrifice. Stalin and his régime systematically "shielded" Soviet citizens from knowledge of the outside world, by censorship, by cutting off personal contacts, by misinformation. The need to do so, in their eyes, was greatly increased by the extent of the drop in living standards in the early 'thirties.

But we must now come to Stalin's more direct contribution to the brutality and terrorism of the Stalin era.

There was, firstly, his needless cruelty which showed itself already in the methods used to impose collectivisation. The great purges were surely not "objectively necessary." To explain them one has to take into account Stalin's thirst for supreme power, his intense pathological suspiciousness, *i.e.,* matters pertaining to Stalin's personal position and character. These led him to massacre the majority of the "Stalinist" central committee elected in 1934, who had supported or at the very least tolerated Stalin's policies up to that date. The facts suggest that they believed that relaxation was possible and desirable; many of them seem to have died for the crime of saying so. . . .

. . . One could argue that the myth about "voluntary collectivisation" was an objectively necessary lie, in the sense of transcending Stalin's personality; indeed, this lie figures in the Party programme adopted by the 22nd Congress last November. But Stalin's lies went very much beyond this, and beyond the distortions and myths which can be ascribed to other politicians in other countries.

Throughout Russia, officials at all levels modelled themselves on Stalin, and each succeeded in imposing more unnecessary misery on more subordinates, stultifying initiative, penalising intelligence, discouraging originality. The price of all this is still being paid.

The urgent need to prepare for war has often been advanced as an excuse for Stalin's industrial "tempos" and for the terror. This can hardly be accepted. In the worst years of social coercion and over-ambitious plans, *i.e.*, 1929–33, Hitler was only just climbing to power, and Comintern policy showed that he was not then regarded as the main enemy. It is possible that Stalin was liquidating all potential opponents in the Purges of 1936–38 as a precaution in case war broke out, though this seems doubtful for a variety of reasons. But it is quite false to use the result of the war as ex-post-factum justification of Stalinism. Perhaps, with less harsh policies, the greater degree of loyalty in 1941 would have offset a smaller industrial base? In any event the Purges not only led to the slaughter of the best military officers but also halted the growth of heavy industry.

The attentive reader will have noticed that this analysis has some features in common with Khrushchev's. Before 1934, Stalin had been carrying out policies which commanded the assent of a majority of the Party and which, like collectivisation, had been accepted as necessary and irreversible by the bulk of Party members, whatever their reservations about particular mistakes and acts of brutality. However, after that date he took more and more personal, arbitrary measures, massacred much of the Party, behaved like an oriental despot. It is true that he was also arbitrary before 1934, and that he took some wise decisions after that date; but there is a case for placing a qualitative change around then.

But this is by no means the end of the matter. It is not only a question of making some obvious remarks concerning Khrushchev's own role during the terror. Of much more general significance is the fact that the events prior to 1934, including the building-up of Stalin into an all-powerful and infallible dictator (by men many of whom he afterwards massacred), cannot be disassociated with what followed; at the very least they provided Stalin with his opportunity. This is where the historian must avoid the twin and opposite pitfalls of regarding what happened as inevitable, and regarding it as a chapter of "personalised" accidents. At each stage there are choices to be made, though the range of possible choices is generally much narrower than people suppose. In 1928 any practicable Bolshevik programme would have been harsh and unpopular. It might not have been *so* harsh and unpopular but for choices which need not necessarily have been made. If before 1934, *i.e.*, in the very period of maximum social coercion, Stalin truly represented the will of the Party, and Khrushchev argues that he did, some totalitarian consequences logically follow. One of these, as already suggested, is the semi-militarised party led by a *Fuehrer*, a dictator, because without an unquestioned leader the consequences of the policies adopted could not be faced.

But, even if it is true that the triumph of a dictator may be explained by objective circumstances which certainly existed in the Soviet situation, the acts of a dictator once he has "arrived" involve a considerable (though of course not infinite) degree of personal choice. Those who gave him the opportunity to act in an arbitrary and cruel way, who adopted policies which involved arbitrariness and coercion on a big scale, cannot ascribe subsequent events to the wickedness of one man or his immediate associates and claim that their hands are clean, even indeed if they were shot themselves on Stalin's orders. The whole-hog Stalin, in other words, was not "necessary," but the possibility of a Stalin was a necessary consequence of the effort of a minority group to keep power and to carry out a vast social-economic revolution in a very short time. And *some* elements of Stalinism were, in those circumstances, scarcely avoidable.

The serious problem for us is to see how far certain elements of Stalinism, in the sense of purposefully-applied social coercion, imposed by a party in the name of an ideology, are likely or liable to accompany rapid economic development even in non-Communist countries.

For it is surely true that many of the problems tackled by Stalin so brutally are present elsewhere, though events in the U.S.S.R. were, of course, deeply affected by peculiar features of Russia and of Bolshevism. The West should indeed emphasise the high cost in human and material terms of a Stalin, and show that the rise of such a man to supreme power in the Soviet Union was, to use the familiar Soviet-Marxist jargon phrase, "not accidental." Indeed, some Western historians who normally write "personalist" and empiricist history will begin to see the virtues of an approach they normally deride as "historicist"; they will analyse Soviet history to establish patterns, regularities, "necessities" which lead to Stalin. By contrast, an embarrassed Khrushchev will be — is being — forced to give an un-Marxist emphasis to personal and accidental factors.

But, of course, we must not confine our search for "necessities" in history only to instances which happen to serve a propagandist purpose. This would be a typically Soviet approach to historiography, only in reverse. It is particularly important to think very seriously about the inter-relationship of coercion and industrialisation, about the nature of the obstacles and vicious circles which drive men to think in totalitarian terms. Unless we realise how complex are the problems which development brings, how irrelevant are many of our ideas to the practical possibilities open to statesmen in these countries, we may unconsciously drive them towards the road which led to Stalin. They cannot be satisfied with "the pace of a tortoise."

III. THE SOCIAL COUNTERREVOLUTION

The Renovation of Bureaucracy

BARRINGTON MOORE

Barrington Moore (1913–   ), Professor of Sociology at Harvard University, has written extensively on the structure and development of the Soviet government and society. His first major work was an analysis of the real trends of social change in Russia and their divergence from the Marxist ideal. In particular he found that by the time of the Stalin Revolution Soviet society was clearly based on a bureaucratic hierarchy of skill and responsibility.

EARLY FUMBLINGS

In the absence of an adequate skill group, the old Tsarist bureaucracy managed to hang on to a surprising extent. A valuable Soviet account published in 1932 reveals that in some sections of the bureaucracy as high as 50 per cent of the personnel were former Tsarist officials. Instances were likewise uncovered about this time of the patterning of Soviet administrative decrees on Tsarist models. This situation prevailed in spite of fairly intensive efforts to replace the old Tsarist bureaucracy with workers and peasants and to build up a new Soviet intelligentsia, efforts that before the Stalinist regime evidently enjoyed only limited success in limited fields, despite earlier claims to the contrary. In addition, the Bolsheviks in the beginning drew fairly heavily for scientific and technical skills on the pre-revolutionary intelligentsia, though important elements in the Party were strongly opposed to pampering the specialists or *spets,* as they were usually called. Lenin was frequently forced to intervene on their behalf. Probably one reason that made it possible to use these individuals was that a considerable section of the intelligentsia had been opposed to the old regime and was aware of its inefficiencies.

Figures on the total size of the Soviet bureaucracy prior to the Stalinist regime are not easy to find. In 1925 Molotov revealed in his report to the Fourteenth Party Congress that there had been a 10 per cent increase in the government personnel, which then numbered 1,850,000 persons. In 1926, according to the *Large Soviet Encyclopedia,* the bureaucracy of the entire soviet apparatus included 2,500,000 people. For a regime which had come to power on the program of destroying bureaucracy, and which continued to give lip service to this idea into the early 1930's this was a sizable figure.

DECISION-MAKING: INEQUALITIES OF POWER

Under the conditions of the Civil War various conceptions of democratic management of industry, of which workers' control had been merely an extreme manifestation, had to give way in practice to a bureaucratic management, exercised through special officials. Returning the factories to their owners was, of course, out of the question for political and mili-

Reprinted by permission of the author and publishers from Barrington Moore, *Soviet Politics — the Dilemma of Power: The Role of Ideas in Social Change.* Cambridge, Mass.: Harvard University Press, 1950 (Russian Research Center Studies, no. 2); Copyright by the President and Fellows of Harvard College. Pp. 163–171, 182–188.

tary reasons; nevertheless, about one fifth of them, particularly those concerned with war industries, continued during the first months of the new regime to work under their old ownership and management.

By about 1919 the prevailing practice in management consisted of collegiums or boards composed of two-thirds workers and one-third engineers or technicians approved by the trade union. Even this diffusion of responsibility led to enormous difficulties. According to Soviet authors, during the period of War Communism the transition from a system of broad representative collegiums to a system of small workers' collectives or even individual responsibility and one-man management made considerable headway. By 1920, 85 per cent of the enterprises in the new regime were controlled by individual managers, though the powers of these managers were still weak and subject to marked interference by other organs representing the interests of the workers or the state.

During 1920 there was considerable discussion in high Party circles concerning the problems of democratic management. The trade-union leader, M. Tomsky, and members of the Workers' Opposition defended collegial management as the only method capable of achieving broad mass participation in the management of industry. They asserted that one-man management was not up to handling the complex problems of the day. Other arguments adduced in support of collegial management asserted that it provided the only way through which the proletariat could learn to take over real control of the country.

Lenin repudiated these views in blunt language. He told the Ninth Party Congress in the spring of 1920, "You cannot escape . . . by declaring that corporate management is a school of government . . . You cannot stay forever in the preparatory class of a school. That will not do. We are now grown up, and we shall be beaten and beaten again in every field, if we behave like school children."

The sharpness of this repudiation is striking. Quite frequently Communist ideals that could not be achieved at the time were put into cold storage to be realized at some distant and undefined future. An example of this type is the "withering away of the state." But in the case of the specific institutional form of collegial management, Lenin refused to regard it even as a goal. Instead, he spoke of it as something embryonic, essential only in the first stage of construction when it was necessary to build anew. But in the transition to practical work, one-man-management, he asserted, made the best use of human skills.

The Congress did not go as far as Lenin in the repudiation of the collegial principle. It adopted instead a compromise resolution, declaring that although the collegial principle had a place in the process of reaching decisions, it should without question give place to individual responsibility in the execution of decisions.

The conflict between collectivist and individual conceptions continued for many years afterward. The official line swung back and forth between two extremes. In general, the collegial principle was more widely retained in the upper branches of the government, where matters of policy were considered, while the principle of individual responsibility was increasingly applied at the level of factory management, where the situation involved more the execution than the formulation of policy.

Both the conceptions and the practice of democratic administration were further modified through the gradual elimination of the influence of the trade unions in matters directly associated with the management of the economy. The initiative in this movement came from the top ranks of the trade-union bureaucracy, which was closely connected with the Party. In the spring of 1920 Tomsky declared that the trade unions should not interfere directly in the problems of management. It was sufficient, he stated, that the unions were represented in the economic organs of the state and participated in the problems of management through these organs. This move may well have been an effort on the part of the trade-union leaders to strengthen their position vis-à-vis their followers. The Ninth Congress of the Party in the same year gave the *coup de grâce* to the doctrines and institutions of workers' control by declaring that the factory committees should not interfere in management. The blow was partly softened by the Party declaration that the unions should concentrate on the task of preparing officer cadres for industry from among the workers by means of professional and technical education.

Two years later the Eleventh Party Congress repeated this formula in even stronger terms, declaring that any immediate interference of the unions in the management of the factory must be considered without qualification harmful and impermissible. Early in the same year (1922), the Trade Unions Congress declared that the unions must give up the principle of equal rights in the naming of industrial managers and other officials concerned with economic administration. In this fashion most of the power over the selection of industrial leadership, as well as over the latter's day-to-day decisions, was taken away from the unions and turned over to the organs of economic administration. For the remainder of the NEP period the Communists kept to this arrangement.

One aspect of the pattern of collective decision-making, which gave the unions a certain limited power in the administration of the factory, remained in force until well into the thirties. This was the so-called "triangle," composed of the plant manager, the trade-union organization or workers' plant committee, and the Party cell within the plant. A struggle for power among these three elements took place all during the twenties. According to Soviet sources, the plant management frequently censored the wall newspaper of the workers, the Party cell tried to decide questions of a purely business nature, and the trade-union group would do the same thing,

forgetting all about its tasks as a union organization.

In September of 1929 a Party decree attempted to set up a system of one-man management in the factory, which, though neither the first nor the last decision of its kind, may be regarded as official recognition that the triangle arrangement was unsatisfactory. Subsequently complaints continued to the effect that authority and responsibility were still divided. It was not until 1937 that a top Party officer, Zhdanov, could declare that the triangle had no more justification for existing.

During the NEP there was a definite conflict between the requirements of efficiency, or what Bukharin had called the logic of the production process, and the goals of the Communist Party. Preobrazhensky put his finger on the difficulty, pointing out that under the NEP, in which government and private industry competed to a considerable extent, the socialist managers who were able to operate their plants with the greatest possible profit might not be the ones who were doing the Party and the working class the most good on a long-run basis. Since labor conditions were frequently better in the privately owned and managed plants than in those operated by the regime, the situation contained a threat to the Party's leadership of the industrial workers.

In addition, certain circles in business administration began to express ideas similar to the conservative American view of "more business in government and less government in business." These groups gathered around Krassin, an old Bolshevik with considerable business experience from prerevolutionary times. Though Krassin denied some of the ideas attributed to him, he stressed the need for good Party administrators, organizers, and managers in the course of sharp debates on this question at the Twelfth Party Congress. About this time he is said to have complained that the top Party leaders were the same as they had been two decades previously, "newspaper dilletantes and litterateurs," who interfered in the choice of business personnel without knowing anything about the subject.

Not all the directors sought power, of course. Some found it more advantageous to avoid responsibility, taking advantage of the triangle or other similar institutions, in the hope of escaping direct accountability for decisions that might involve disastrous personal consequences. Nevertheless, the problem continued to cause difficulties down to the beginning of the Five Year Plans. As late as 1929 one of the Party leaders brought up at a Party Conference the case of a prominent trust director with a good reputation for efficiency who complained of "too much control — the Workers' and Peasants' Inspection and the unions get in the way."

Until the complete change of policy involved in the rapid industrialization and extension of Party control under the Five Year Plans, there was very little the Party could do about this situation. On the whole, it endeavored to solve the dilemma during the NEP by strengthening the power of the managers and backing them up with the weapon of high-policy declarations. In defining the duties and functions of the director, the Party declared that his main job was to increase the productivity of labor, lower the cost of production, and increase the quantity of material goods available for the workers' government. In 1924 the Party declared that the local Party leaders must give the managers full support and must not permit them to be disturbed by minor distractions. Furthermore, the Party during this time gradually managed to create its own managerial group. Some interesting figures on this point were presented by Kaganovich at the Sixteenth Party Congress in 1930. He reported, on the basis of a sample of about 1300 factory directors, that 29 per cent of the directors were Party members in 1923, 48 per cent in 1924, and 93 per cent in 1929. In this way the factory directors obtained status not only as administrators, but also as Party members. From 1929

onward the state extended its control over all sectors of the economy, eliminating the problem of competition with private industry. By these devices many of the difficulties produced by the objective necessity for status differentials and the goals of Communist policy were solved.

ROLE OF THE EQUALITARIAN MYTH IN THE EXECUTION OF DECISIONS

It is a commonplace observation that making policy is much easier than executing it. Most organized human groupings, and particularly such large ones as the modern state, have had to evolve methods for coping with this problem. They have developed a wide variety of formal and informal techniques for seeing to it that the decisions made by those in authority are at least partly carried out by those subject to authority.

In a socialist society these difficulties tend to be more severe than they do in a free-enterprise system. Under a capitalist regime the decisions about what goods should be produced, and how labor, plant, and raw materials should be efficiently combined to produce them, are largely left to the individual producer, who guides himself by the indexes of cost and selling price. On the other hand, a socialist economy must control deliberately and consciously this range of decisions, instead of leaving them to the free play of market forces. In the latter situation the checks of consumer resistance and the spurs of consumer demand play a much less significant role.

As an excellent English economic historian of the Soviet regime[1] has pointed out, the Soviet administrative problem was enormously magnified from the very beginning by the disappearance of market price as an indicator of what to produce, and in what quantities. For a time military needs took the place of market price. Certain war industries were selected for shock treatment while other subordinate plants

[1] Maurice Dobb. [Editor's note.]

were neglected. When the Civil War ended, and military needs no longer were the major criterion for production and consumption, the system broke down. It had to be replaced by the semi-market economy of the NEP.

Furthermore, a state dominated by a single political party lacks many of the devices for checking up on the execution of decisions that are found in states with competing political parties. In a state with the latter type of political organization, the party that is temporarily in power can be sure that its opponents will be on the lookout for any signs of incompetence in the execution of policy.

The preceding observations do not imply that a socialist or a one-party state is necessarily less efficient in the utilization of human and material resources than a multi-party and capitalist state. Too, the proposition is yet to be proved that a socialist state is necessarily a totalitarian state, even though definite pressures in this direction must be recognized. The point to be made is that for a number of reasons the Soviet regime faced an extraordinarily difficult problem in developing adequate techniques for verifying the execution of policy decisions. As one illustration among many of the scope of the problem, an administrative house cleaning in the Gosplan in March 1931 uncovered 190 unfulfilled orders issued by the government, some of which were almost three years old. These problems were not only the product of the new social system the Soviets were endeavoring to establish. They were also the product of history and the cultural traditions of Russia, which did not include the precise and punctual execution of bureaucratic orders.

On the whole, the problem of execution has been met by setting one part of the bureaucracy to watch another part. Quite a number of different organizations have been established at various times for this specific purpose. For a while this was the chief purported function of the Workers' and Peasants' Inspection. The Party

Control Commissions, and particularly the Central Control Commission . . . fulfilled a number of functions of checking up on the execution of decisions. After 1930 these mechanisms were overhauled and extended with results that will be considered later.

Perhaps the most important role in the task of verifying the execution of major policy decisions has fallen to the secret police. Despite the lack of quantitative data, Simon Liberman's memoirs and other sources show that the secret police expanded rapidly into the economic field in the search for sabotage. The distinctions among deliberate sabotage, administrative incompetence, and reaction to hostile local pressures are difficult enough to draw in any case, and it was not to be expected that the secret police would be overly meticulous in drawing them.

Under such pressures administrative errors tended to become not only criminal offenses but also, under the watchful eye of the Party, to partake of the nature of counterrevolutionary sin. The resulting stifling of initiative and high degree of insecurity on the part of administrative officials have been dramatized in a number of accounts by individuals who have turned against the regime and fled. The extent to which this factor has affected efficiency cannot be measured, though it is unquestionably important.

Partly because the major way of verifying administrative performance lay in the creation of competing bureaucratic elements, the Soviet bureaucracy prior to the Stalinist regime did not develop into a homogeneous unit. There were a number of intense struggles between various sections of the bureaucracy, some of which were conducted mainly behind the scenes. At various times the Red Army showed signs of restiveness and tended to become an independent sector of the bureaucracy, despite the efforts of the Party to keep it under control. Likewise, many of the internecine Party struggles were reflected in the Army. Between 1928 and 1930 the trade-union leadership opposed Stalin's policies associated with rapid industrialization. Stalin was compelled to turn nearly all the top leaders out of office and replace them with his own supporters. The Party itself during this period was not a homogeneous group and was rent by serious divergencies over matters of major policy prior to Stalin's accession to power. . . .

In the attempt to resolve the conflict of interests between the workers and the bureaucracy, Soviet official ideology underwent two major changes. One was the return in the late twenties and early thirties to the doctrines that were promulgated during the period of War Communism. While this return was a widespread, though not universal, feature of the times, it is most striking in respect to the doctrine of no class struggle. When faced with a crisis situation, the regime went back to a familiar symbolism. Freudian notions of "regression" need not be called upon to explain this phenomenon, since the political and economic problems faced during War Communism and the years of the Stalinist Revolution were similar in a number of essential respects. In the second place, one may take note of the utilization of the more "idealistic" aspects of the Marxist-Leninist tradition, that is, the doctrine that the workers were the masters of their own fate, to support a highly authoritarian regime.

THE REPUDIATION OF EQUALITY

The prerevolutionary Bolshevik attitude toward inequalities of wealth was an ambivalent and uncertain one. Like Marx before him, Lenin felt that certain inequalities might remain in the early stages as socialism emerged with violent birth pangs from the womb of capitalism. But he had not hesitated to affirm the eventual goal of equality. In general, the feeling was strong among the early Bolsheviks in both prerevolutionary and postrevolutionary days that inequality was somehow wrong and immoral, a temporary evil that would only have to be endured for a time. There

was no realization that inequalities might be a permanent social necessity as part of a system of incentives to labor.

The idealistic equalitarian point of view remained strong during the period of War Communism. The first program of the Bolsheviks following the November Revolution, adopted at the Eighth Party Congress in March 1919, proclaimed that among the outstanding tasks of the moment was the ideological and educational work required "to destroy completely all traces of previous inequality or prejudices, especially among the backward strata of the proletariat and the peasantry." In accordance with Lenin's and Marx's earlier writings, the authors of the program acknowledged that equality could not be brought about at once, but chose this propitious moment to reaffirm the goal: "While aspiring to equality of remuneration for all kinds of labor and to total Communism, the Soviet government cannot consider as its immediate task the realization of this equality at the present moment, when only the first steps are being made towards the transition from capitalism to Communism."

During the period of War Communism both doctrinal considerations and the necessities of wartime siege favored equality in the distribution of goods and incomes, even though it was an equality perilously close to the zero point. Inequalities remained in the payment of the *spets* or vital technical personnel, inequalities that many Party leaders regarded as purely temporary concessions. In addition, there was a rough system of priorities in the distribution of consumers' goods to the workers in different industries, as well as to different plants within an industry. But by 1920 rationed goods and services distributed free of charge, which constituted almost the sole income of the wage earner, were distributed equally among the workers of any one enterprise. The use of apartments was free, as were theater and tramway tickets.

Not until the spring of 1920 did it apparantly occur to the Communist leaders that equality might result in a loss of production, when production was vital to the survival of the regime. At this time Tomsky, the trade-union leader, declared that the payment of labor ought to depend immediately upon the results of labor. At this time also the Ninth Party Congress went far enough to declare that an incentive system of payments ought to be one of the most powerful means for awakening competition, and even announced that a good worker should be better supplied with the necessities of life than a negligent worker. This line of thinking received a marked impetus with the transition to the NEP and the general overhauling of economic incentives in March 1921. Lenin himself declared in October of the same year that "every important branch of national economy must be built up on the principle of personal incentive."

By the end of the NEP underlying economic factors, together with the Communist retreat from their equalitarian position, had produced a situation in which variations in wage payments did not differ very markedly from corresponding differentials in capitalist countries at a similar stage of economic development. On the basis of careful and detailed study of variations in wage rates, Abram Bergson has concluded that the "capitalist" principles of supply and demand were the fundamental factors determining wage differentials in the Soviet Union during this period. In other words, these differentials depended primarily upon the productivity of different workers. In the month of March 1928 the earnings of workers varied from less than 30 rubles to more than 250 rubles. Six per cent of the wage earners earned less than 30.01 rubles; only 0.2 per cent earned more than 250 rubles. However, the wages of 47.9 per cent of the earners varied between the rather narrow range of 40 to 80 rubles. Though the variation or inequality of wages in the Soviet Union in 1928 was less than had

been the case in Russia in 1914, the differences were slight.

Wages are by themselves not a completely accurate index of variations in real income, owing to the number of services provided for the workers by government and civic organizations for the improvement of material and cultural living standards. In the Soviet Union these extra factors are important at all income levels, because of the practice of giving responsible officials houses, the use of automobiles for official purposes, and the like. Furthermore, figures on wages do not cover more than a fraction of the population. Therefore, figures on the distribution of savings, available for 1930, provide a welcome addition to those on wages. Total savings in the hands of the banks in that year amounted to 722 million rubles. They were allegedly distributed in the following proportions:

Workers	91 million
Clerical workers and members of the bureaucracy	205 million
Others (professional men, craftsmen, etc.)	134 million
Individual peasants	46 million
Collective farms and other "juristic persons"	246 million

Even though this information may arouse rather than satisfy curiosity at many points, it is plain that the Soviet system had by this time developed a system of organized social inequality with marked similarities to that in capitalist societies.

In response to forces beyond their control, the equalitarian idealists in the Party were compelled to compromise and rationalize at several points. For example, in 1929 the rule limiting members of the Party to a maximum income was modified to exclude from its limitations several of the major occupations in which it was possible to earn more than the legally defined maximum. It may also be significant that the maximum itself was not indicated in this decree.

Nevertheless, the period of the twenties was not one of complete retreat from the equalitarian position. Latent pressures among the industrial workers helped to keep the tradition alive. It showed some vitality in high Party circles down to the time of Stalin's caustic repudiation in 1931.

Factory workers, particularly those at the lowest paid level, were suffering in 1925 and afterward under the impact of monetary inflation, which gave rise to demands for an upward leveling of wage rates. Likewise, there were objections among the workers to the use of incentive differentials as a whip to increase production. This was particularly strong among small groups of workers in continual face-to-face contact, who objected to what they felt were injustices in differing rates of payment for fairly similar tasks. The situation was exacerbated by the attempts of the Left Opposition to capitalize on this discontent. On this account the Party approved, in November 1926, a rise in wage rates as the "first and an important step in the direction of eliminating the plainly abnormal differences in pay among various categories of workers." Similarly, at the Seventh Congress of Trade Unions in December 1926, Tomsky spoke of the gap between the wages of skilled and unskilled labor, which supposedly violated prevailing conceptions of "elementary class justice," a tribute to the continuing equalitarian tradition. "In the future we must reduce the gap in wages between qualified and ordinary labor," he concluded. Actually, a widespread revision of wage scales, which resulted in some diminution of inequalities, was undertaken at that time under the supervision of the All-Union Central Council of Trade Unions.

These events may be regarded as the last flicker of the equalitarian tradition, at least in official circles — a final effort to achieve equality of rewards for all. Not long after the drive for industrialization, embodied in the First Five Year Plan, had

gotten under way, Stalin removed Tomsky from the leadership of the trade unions and specifically repudiated his conception of "elementary class justice."

Speaking in 1931, Stalin pointed out that while the Plan called for an over-all increase of industrial production of 31 to 32 per cent in 1930, the actual increase amounted to only 25 per cent. In the key industries of coal mining, iron, and steel, the increase was only from 6 to 10 per cent. Obviously, the objectives of the Communist leadership were in serious danger.

A major line of attack lay in the overhauling of the wage system, one of the central features of Stalin's policy. Commenting on the heavy turnover in the labor force, Stalin said:

The cause is the wrong structure of wages, the wrong wage scales, the "Leftist" practice of wage equalization. In a number of our factories wage scales are drawn up in such a way as to practically wipe out the difference between skilled labour and unskilled labour, between heavy work and light work. The consequence of wage equalization is that the unskilled worker lacks the incentive to become a skilled worker and is thus deprived of the prospect of advancement; as a result he feels himself a "sojourner" in the factory, working only temporarily so as to earn a little and then go off to "seek his fortune" elsewhere.

These remarks were dinned into the consciousness of Soviet citizens by every means of communication at the Party's disposal. Stalin emphasized what Lenin had merely suggested — that inequality served a necessary social function in a socialist as well as in a capitalist society. It is this point which constitutes a new element in Russian Marxist ideology, and which serves as the basis for the contemporary justification of organized social inequality.

The Stalinist slogan for the system of distribution under socialism: "From each according to his abilities, to each according to his labor." Equality is stigmatized as "petty bourgeois." The goal remains that proclaimed by Marx: a higher (Communist) form of society in which the slogan "From each according to his abilities, to each according to his *needs*" will supposedly prevail. Older Bolshevik theorists, perhaps not in accord with the strictest logic, interpreted the latter to mean equality of rewards for all. Such interpretations are now conspicuous by their absence.

There is a significant contrast between the fate of early doctrines concerning equality of power and similar doctrines concerning equality of rewards. In practice, inequalities developed rapidly in both areas. On the basis of various prerevolutionary features of Bolshevik ideology and behavior, that is, the theory and practice of a conspiratorial elite, the stage was set to an important extent for the development of inequalities of power. At the same time, the concurrent stream of ideas to the effect that the new regime would be sensitive to the needs of the masses, that it would represent the highest expression of the will of the toilers, and the masses would soon be the masters of their fate, was retained and in some respects even amplified to give a further atmosphere of legitimacy, consensus, and mass support to the new regime. On the other hand, the conception of equality of rewards was repudiated as incompatible with the major goal of industrialization, or at best allowed to slip into forgetfulness as a possible feature of an indefinite future. The difference between the fate of the two sets of ideas may perhaps be explained as a consequence of the differing social function each set could play under the new social conditions.

The Repudiation of Experiment

GEORGE S. COUNTS

George S. Counts (1889–   ), Professor at Teachers College, Columbia University, is a long-standing authority on education in the Soviet Union. In the historical section of his most recent work he describes the drastic changes made in Soviet educational policy in the early 1930's. This was part of the general movement by Stalin and his supporters to put an end to the radical cultural and social experiments of the 1920's and institute more traditional and highly disciplinarian standards instead.

Soviet educators have called the period from 1921 to 1931 the "experimental" period in the history of Soviet education. It might also be called the "romantic" period. And the student of Soviet politics might with good reason call it the period of the capture of the school, the pupil, and the teacher by the Party. At any rate, during these years the mastery of knowledge was clearly subordinated to the political education of the younger generation. The Party did not give the close attention to details of school management that characterized the later period. To be sure, it endorsed certain broad conceptions of education, such as the "unified labor school" and "polytechnical education," to which it gave the Marxian label. But this

With permission of McGraw-Hill Book Co., Inc. from *The Challenge of Soviet Education* by George S. Counts (New York: 1957), pp. 60–65, 68–74. Copyright © 1957 by the McGraw-Hill Book Company, Inc.

left broad areas in which educators and teachers could conduct discussions, engage in experimentation, and espouse divergent approaches to educational tasks and objectives. Moreover, the Soviet educator took pride in his knowledge of the educational ideas and practices of capitalist countries. There was abundant evidence in the 1920s of the persisting influence of the liberal and humanist movement of the two preceding generations.

Several of the leading educators of the period had actually worked in this movement. N. K. Krupskaia, wife and widow of Lenin, and head of the important department of political education of the Commissariat of Education, had taught in the Sunday schools before the revolution. Invariably she impressed all who came to know her as a person of deep human sympathies. Albert Pinkevich, whose books on the theory and practice of education were widely used in teacher-training institutions, had been principal of a secondary school for boys in St. Petersburg which was renowned for its progressive methods — progressive in the Western meaning of the word. And then there was S. T. Shatsky, a remarkable personality who had been influenced by Jane Addams and John Dewey and who after the revolution was appointed head of the First Experimental Station in People's Education in Moscow. All these persons, and many others, had experienced harsh treatment at the hands of the Russian autocracy. Little wonder that they interpreted the revolution as a sort of key to the gates of an educational paradise. In his memoirs Shatsky contrasted the old school which he had attended as a boy with the new school of the Soviet regime. The former was marked by harsh discipline, mastery of subject matter, and preparation for adult life; the latter, by regard for the child as a human being and the organization of instruction around his current interests. And Paul Blonsky, father of Soviet pedology and author of *The Unified Labor School* published in 1919, was a devout advocate of freedom for the child. An admirer of Rousseau, he suggested that Robinson Crusoe on the desert island provided a sound method for the education of the younger generation. He condemned as "prejudices of the old school" the recitation, the teaching plan, the separate subjects, the gradation of classes, the system of marks, the lack of faith in the child, and the passion for book learning.

In the light of developments in the 1930s, to be reported later, it is important to note that in this period a Soviet educator might express his own ideas and take exception to pronouncements by the state authorities. The case of Pinkevich may serve as an illustration. In his preface to the American edition of his *Outlines of Pedagogy*, which went through several editions in the Russian language, he addresses the following words to the English reader:

I wish to make it perfectly clear . . . that the system expounded in the present book is not the generally accepted system, nor is it the official system. Although the basic principles upon which Soviet educators are striving to build a system of Marxian pedagogy are everywhere the same, there may be wide differences in details and in the handling of individual questions. Moreover, the development of a uniform theory of education is neither possible nor desirable. In the present case it is sufficient to note that my position on fundamental issues is *typical* of the great majority of Soviet educators.

In discussing the Programs of the Primary School prepared by the State Scientific Council of the Commissariat of Education, Pinkevich says that, while they "contain extremely valuable material," they are subject to the "fundamental criticism" of violating the "principle of objective teaching." After giving an example, he argues that there is "danger of the blind acceptance on faith of the dogmatic statements of the instructor" and that in "our opinion the entire program is threatened with dogmatization." He disappeared in the purges of 1937.

In this period there was widespread interest in the development of education in other lands. A writer in the field of pedagogy would invariably present the theories of leading educators in Europe and America, and do so in a friendly spirit and with a considerable measure of objectivity. Thus Pinkevich could say that he found the works of American educators "a rich source of materials" and "the most valuable source" from beyond the borders of the Soviet Union. Also, after reviewing the ideas of leading Western educators, he speaks of "the great American philosopher, John Dewey," and ranks him "among the bourgeois forerunners of the true labor school." And Blonsky, perhaps the most erudite Soviet scholar in the whole field of education, followed very closely the work of E. L. Thorndike, Charles H. Judd, and others. Incidentally, his subject of pedology was declared a pseudo science by the Central Committee of the Party in 1936. The subject was forthwith abolished and Blonsky disappeared. A. V. Lunacharsky, a friend of Lenin and the first Commissar of Education in the Russian Republic, was something of a cosmopolitan, a man of broad cultural interests, a connoisseur and patron of the arts who intervened with Lenin at the time of the revolution to save from destruction the art treasures of old Russia. In 1928,[1] four years after the death of Lenin, he was removed from office. A visitor to the Soviet Union in the 1920s was generally impressed by the eagerness of Soviet teachers and educators to learn about educational practices in other lands. As a rule, however, they would state explicitly that the techniques, and not the purposes, of education in capitalist countries would be of value to them.

The school which these people and their collaborators built under the directives issued by the Party was called the "unified labor school." It was "unified" because it was organized at three levels as a single school, with provision for the unimpeded progress of the child from the first grade to the ninth or tenth. It was

called "labor" because in Marxian theory human labor is the source of all value and the laboring class is the builder of the new society. Thus labor is endowed with that mystical quality in a Communist order which marks the role of the proletariat in the history of the present epoch. By labor even a member of the despised bourgeoisie may redeem himself and become whole. And so the education of the young must be linked with labor as theory must be linked with practice, words with deeds. Here, the Soviet leaders contended, was the greatest and most fruitful invention in the whole history of education, but an invention which could be put to use only under the rule of the proletariat.

This school was an activity school, a school in which children learned by doing. In contrasting their school with the school of the past, the Soviet educators were fond of saying that their school was a "school that does" rather than a "school that talks." But the word "activity" in the Soviet context was given a meaning which distinguished it radically from that prevailing in the so-called progressive schools of the West. It carried a moral and social content. As one enthusiast said, "The question of 'the socially useful activities of the school' must be regarded at the present moment as the most important question of Soviet pedagogy, because it constitutes the sharpest and brightest trait which distinguishes the Soviet school, not only from the tsarist school, but also from every other contemporary school." The Soviet school must be as "bright and unique" as the "Soviet Union which gave it birth." And this basic characteristic is not found in the "complex method, self-government, or the social work of the teacher. Relatively speaking, all of these are trivialities." The Soviet school, "being created in the epoch of the stupendous sweep of a program for building the country, *must itself participate in the building of life.*" In a word, education must be a central factor in the direct transformation of both man and society. . . .

[1] Actually 1929. [Editor's note.]

The point should be emphasized that socially useful labor was not merely a method of teaching. Nor was it a substitute for the traditional curriculum. As a matter of fact, it was both method and curriculum. In the opinion of Soviet educators it added content and gave vitality to the entire program of instruction. The school continued to teach the native tongue, natural science, social studies, and mathematics, but it did all these things in relation to contemporary life and the tasks of Soviet society as determined by the Bolshevik dictatorship. Socially useful labor gave a new dimension to the curriculum and profoundly altered its structure. The mastery of academic subjects as such was relegated to a subordinate position. Some Soviet educators contended that subjects should be abolished and that the child should acquire necessary skills and knowledges as a by-product of the pursuit of socially desirable ends. This led to the development of interest in the "method of projects" and convinced many American visitors that the Bolsheviks had adopted the philosophy and program of "progressive education." The Soviet educators also were attracted to the "Dalton plan" and the "laboratory method," not only for the natural sciences, but also for other subjects. One of the most enthusiastic advocates of socially useful labor was V. N. Shul'gin, director of the Institute of School Methods in Moscow. Taking seriously the Marxian prophecy that the state would "wither away" after the establishment of socialism and confident that socialism was not far away, he developed and expounded the doctrine of the "withering away of the school." He saw the child of the future acquiring his education by participating in the life of society, each of whose institutions would perform its appropriate educational function. The child would grow up, "not in a school, not in a kindergarten, not in a retort of a chemical laboratory," but in the "factory, the mill, the agricultural economy, the class struggle." And he would be taught, "not by a teacher in a box, in a knit cap," but "by the entire order of things." Also, "industry will be placed at the service of education. It will be organized for educational purposes, as will be the street." According to a report received by the writer in Moscow in 1936, Shul'gin himself was at that time "withering away" on an engineering project in the region of the North Caucasus. And he was not serving as an engineer. . . .

With the launching of the great program for the industrialization of the country in the autumn of 1928 and the complete triumph of Stalin over his rivals by the early thirties, the so-called "experimental period" came to a close. The educational practices of that period had been at least measurably successful in the propagation of Bolshevik doctrines among children and youth. Many of the old teachers had been either reconciled with the revolution or eliminated from the profession by natural or political causes. As early as June 12, 1925, the Soviet of People's Commissars of the RSFSR [2] "notices a considerable improvement in the ideas and attitudes of the body of teachers toward the new regime," and "a parallel improvement of the same order generally among scientists." Also a new generation of teachers, reared in large part under Soviet institutions and presumably loyal to the regime, was emerging. At the same time, the program of construction carried through in the early years with the assistance of foreign engineers, technicians, and even skilled workers, called for the swift mastery of science and technology. As a consequence, novel and exacting demands were made on the schools. They were asked to participate actively in the conversion of a technically and culturally backward country into a modern industrial state. In 1936, when the author inquired of teachers and children in both European Russia and Siberia regarding the first duty of the

[2] RSFSR: The Russian Socialist Federated Soviet Republic, the original Communist state of 1917 and the main constituent republic of the Union of Soviet Socialist Republics after the latter was formed in 1922. [Editor's note.]

pupil, the response was everywhere the same — "the mastery of knowledge." The immediate fulfillment of the Five-Year Plan was left to the older generation. The pupil's first responsibility was to study language, mathematics, and science. Added to all this was the profound shift in the whole orientation and configuration of Soviet life and institutions associated with the rise of Stalin and Stalinism. In the process of adjustment to the new conditions many of the practices and doctrines of the earlier period were modified, abandoned, or reversed. But only in a limited sense were the issues pedagogical in nature. At bottom, like everything else in the Soviet Union, including the content of the calendar and the humor of the circus, they were essentially political issues — political issues of critical concern to the dictatorship.

The demands of the program of construction and the slogan of overtaking and surpassing the most advanced capitalist countries merit an additional word. As the Soviet leaders struggled to achieve the goals of the First Five-Year Plan, they became painfully aware of the general backwardness of Russia. This they had all said many times; indeed, Soviet literature had been filled with this lament all through the period of the battle to consolidate Bolshevik rule. But only as they undertook the heavy tasks of industrial construction did they realize fully the truth of the oft-repeated indictment of the past. They found to their sorrow that the rank and file of Soviet citizens did indeed lag far behind the peoples of the West in the most elementary mastery of the skills, knowledges, and understandings required in the building of an industrial economy — skills, knowledges, and understandings which the child in America acquires more or less incidentally in the process of growing up amid complicated tools, machines, motors, and electricity. The unified labor school, with its emphasis on socially useful work, freedom from discipline, unorganized curricula, political indoctrination, and

diverse romantic notions about education stemming from Marx and Lenin, simply was not sufficient to the task. As a consequence, practically the entire regimen of the middle school was swiftly transformed by decrees issued either directly or indirectly by the Central Committee of the Party. These decrees were directed, not only to broad educational policies, but also to the details of instruction and school management. As a consequence, a new Soviet school emerged which was profoundly different from the school of the 1920s — a school which resembled in many respects the school of old Russia and would have been labeled counterrevolutionary in the earlier period, but one which in fact expresses the basic philosophy of Bolshevism far more faithfully than its predecessor.

The first of these important decrees, issued on September 5, 1931, called for the simple mastery of knowledge. According to the Central Committee, "the basic defect of our school at the present moment" is the "fact that school instruction fails to give a sufficient body of general knowledge" and thus fails to "prepare for the technicums and higher schools fully literate people with a good command of the basic sciences (physics, chemistry, mathematics, native language, geography and others)." While continuing to stress the principle of "polytechnical education," the decree condemns the traditional practice in these sharp words: "Every attempt to separate the polytechnization of the school from a systematic and firm mastery of the sciences, and of physics, chemistry, and mathematics in particular . . . constitutes the most flagrant perversion of the ideas of the polytechnical school." The teaching of these subjects "must be conducted by means of strictly established schedules." In order to emphasize the importance and urgency of the need for a fundamental reorganization of the entire program of instruction, the Central Committee asked the commissariats of education in the Union Republics "to organize immediately a scientific-Marxian revision of the program, making certain that it contains a strictly defined body of systematic knowledge (native language, mathematics, physics, chemistry, geography, history)." The date for the introduction of the "new revised programs" was set for January 1, 1932. In the meantime, all necessary practical measures were to be taken to instruct the teachers and prepare directives for launching the new programs without delay. To expedite the reforms, "all members of the Party engaged in the work of people's education" were instructed "to master the new procedures in the shortest possible time." Thus was restored the curriculum of separate subjects — subjects with clearly defined content to be mastered by the pupil. And this curriculum was to be uniform for practically all children from the first grade to the tenth.

The decree of September 5, 1931, ordered corresponding changes in the field of methods of instruction. While recognizing the value of some of the new methods of teaching "in the development of initiative and the preparation of active participants in socialist construction," it demanded the launching of a "decisive warfare against irresponsible projectorizing and the introduction on a mass scale of methods untested in practice." This error assumed its most glaring form in the "adoption of the so-called 'project method.' Stemming directly from the anti-Leninist theory of the 'withering away of the school,' the attempts to place the 'project method' at the basis of the entire school acually led to the destruction of the school." It is interesting to note, incidentally, that Krupskaia had been particularly enthusiastic about this method. The Central Committee warned the entire teaching profession against both "extreme left tendencies" and "attempts to go back to the bourgeois school." However, the response to this initial decree was quite unsatisfactory. Consequently, on August 25, 1932, the Central Committee issued another decree, which ordered the "liquida-

tion of the perversions of laboratory-brigade methods" and then proceeded to a positive definition of the appropriate method for the Soviet school: "The chief form of the organization of instruction in the primary and secondary school must be the recitation with a given group of pupils following a strict schedule of studies. Under the leadership of the teacher this form must include group, brigade, and individual work of each pupil," and "the teacher must present the subject he is teaching systematically and consistently."

Implicit in the emphasis on the mastery of knowledge and the revival of the recitation is a fundamental change in the relations between teacher and pupil. The decree of September 5, 1931, called upon the commissariats of education to strengthen "individual authority in the management of the school" and to "increase the responsibility of the teaching body in their work by promoting and encouraging loyal and well-trained teachers." At the same time, "the work of children's self-government in the school" was to be "directed chiefly toward the improvement of the quality of learning and the strengthening of school discipline." The decree may be understood also as marking the emergence of a body of teachers presumably loyal to the regime. . . .

The demand of the Central Committee that the mastery of a definite body of knowledge should be the basic purpose of the middle school led speedily to the reversal of a fairly well established Soviet tradition regarding the role of the textbook in the educative process. Many of the foremost leaders of Soviet education, including Krupskaia, Shatsky, and Blonsky, were fond of saying that "life must be the textbook." This position was officially proclaimed by the Russian Commissariat of Education in the following words contained in a circular letter dated August, 1918: "Textbooks in general should be thrown out of the school." As late as May, 1930, an all-Russian conference of educators "definitely repudiates the principle of the stabilization of text-books." In the same year the Plenum of the Central Committee of the Professional Union of Educational Workers declared that the standardization of textbooks is "incorrect and politically injurious." But on February 12, 1933, the Central Committee of the Party pronounced this attitude toward the textbook "incorrect" and "intolerable." It then proceeded to instruct the Commissariat of Education to prepare "stable textbooks" in the "native language, mathematics, geography, physics, chemistry, biology, etc." And the date of publication was set for "July 15, 1933, in order that they may be ready for the opening of the academic year — September 1, 1933"! In the sense of the Committee, a "stable textbook" is one "designed for use over a period of many years" and "approved after a preliminary scrupulous examination by the Collegium of the Commissariat of Education." In such a textbook, as Stalin once said, "every word and every definition must be weighed." And such a textbook must be prepared for "each subject" taught in the school.

The next step to ensure the mastery of knowledge was the development of a rigorous system of marks, examinations, promotion, and awards. . . .

This transformation of the purposes, the curriculum, and methods of the school was accompanied by an expression of widespread concern regarding the behavior of pupils. From the early thirties the Soviet press contained numerous references to "hooliganism" on the part of children and youth in schools and public places. The general lack of discipline on the part of the young was deplored and a widespread campaign to correct these evils was launched. Even Stalin gave the matter his attention, and the famous cavalry leader, General Budenny, almost a legendary figure, went into the school in 1935 to impress on children the necessity of loving and respecting their teachers and elders. The pupil was told over and over again that his first duty was to study and learn. No longer was he to assume responsibility for running the school, correcting his parents, managing the affairs of the community, or even assisting directly in the great program of construction. He was subjected increasingly to strict supervision in school, at home, and on the street. Moreover, he was held accountable for his successes and failures as an individual.

The Mobilization of Culture

EDWARD J. BROWN

Edward J. Brown (1909–   ), Professor of Russian at Brown University has investigated a crucial period in the history of Soviet cultural policy — the era of the "Revolutionary Association of Proletarian Writers" (RAPP) under the leadership of Leopold Averbakh. The period of RAPP coincided with the Stalin Revolution, and the primary purpose of the organization was to bring Russian writers under Communist Party control and make literature serve the political purposes of the party. Similar steps were taken at this time in most other cultural fields. In every case, however, the work of these early control agencies failed to satisfy the desire of Stalin and the party leadership for more and simpler propaganda. By the mid thirties RAPP and its kindred organizaticns had been dissolved and replaced by new bodies ready to fulfill Stalin's requirements of "socialist realism" without question or complaint.

THE works of Averbakh and the official statements of the leaderhip of RAPP make frequent reference to the necessity for a "cultural revolution." The political revolution and the reorganization of industry and agriculture will be meaningless, they indicate, unless these developments are accompanied by a rise in the cultural level of the working masses. The term "culture" is used in a very broad sense to include not only an increase in the popular utilization of literature and art in all its forms, but most of all a rise in general literacy, in education, and in standards of health and sanitation.

Averbakh's main thesis would appear to be that "the productivity of labor depends not only on the industrialization of the country, but also upon raising the educational and cultural level of the masses." This statement in itself would seem to be fairly obvious and to raise no serious political issues: such a program was, at least in its broad outlines, included in the Party program. But the question is one of emphasis. Averbakh's idea is that industrialization at the tempos contemplated by the program of the Party will be impossible without a continuous and concomitant rise in the cultural level of the masses.

Averbakh was in 1928 extremely dissatisfied with the results so far achieved in this realm. He adduces figures to show that only very little had been done to liquidate illiteracy, to broaden educational services, to improve health, and to extend medical care. From the figures he gives the conclusion is inescapable that the USSR was not only far behind the nations of Central and Eastern Europe, but had not even been able to make significant strides beyond the achievements of tsarist Russia.

He stresses the extreme cultural backwardness of the country by comparison with western nations. Apparently in answer to anticipated arguments, he emphasizes that funds expended for such things as education and health care will also

From Edward J. Brown, *The Proletarian Episode in Russian Literature, 1928–1932* (New York: Columbia University Press, 1953), pp. 60–63, 85–88, 90, 92–93, 220–222. Reprinted by permission of the publisher.

contribute to the rise in production figures, for they will improve the quality of the workers.

He quotes speeches made at the Fifteenth Congress of the Party 1927) by Rykov and Bukharin to the effect that further growth in industrialization must be accompanied by a corresponding rise in the cultural level of the masses. He quotes a speech given at the Moscow Party Conference, at which Bukharin had called for an increase in the funds allocated to cultural work. Averbakh concludes:

It is clear, then, that we are lagging behind culturally and that we must give special attention to the . . . financing of the cultural revolution.

The cultural revolution, as Averbakh understood it, involved deep changes in human beings. Such changes of course presupposed the liquidation of illiteracy and the traditional "darkness" of pre-1917 Russia. But they must go much further:

The cultural revolution is a lengthy epoch during which human material will be transformed, the toiling masses themselves will be reeducated, and a new type of man produced. In this work a great and serious task falls to the lot of art, with its specific means of influencing the whole human psyche.

Echoing the conclusions of Averbakh in the brochure quoted above, the resolutions of the RAPP executive emphasize that this cultural work cannot wait for the consolidation of a firm material base for the new society, but must go hand in hand with it. A leading article in one of the early issues of On Literary Guard, printed in large type and apparently designed as a major statement of editorial policy, emphasizes that the Party and the government cannot wait for the outcome of "socialist construction" and the raising of the material level of the workers before interesting themselves in cultural matters. Cultural progress must go hand in hand with construction, or else the latter will be hampered.

The theoreticians and practitioners of proletarian literature believed that their product should be an important agency of this "cultural revolution." The resolution adopted by the First Congress of Proletarian Writers in 1928 sets forth such ideas in the Marxist jargon of the day:

Being one of the means for the cognition of social life and of the whole world which surrounds man, art organizes the feelings and thoughts by means of images influencing the psyche of the reader, listener, etc., through "emotional infection." In the conditions of a class society art is a mighty weapon of the class struggle. In actively influencing all ideological fields, the proletariat makes no exception of art. Therefore one of the main tasks of the cultural revolution is to aid the development of proletarian art and its advanced detachment, proletarian literature.

"To aid the development of . . . proletarian literature," such is the important task of the "cultural revolution." What exactly was understood by the term "proletarian literature"? There is never any question in the statements of RAPP theoreticians on this subject that the term must include not only the literary product of people who are proletarian in origin but also that of nonproletarians who sympathize with — "take the viewpoint of" — the proletariat. And indeed it could not be otherwise, for the leadership of RAPP and a large proportion of its membership were made up of writers and critics who were not of working-class origin. Averbakh, Libedinskii, Fadeev, Panfërov, Kirshon, Gladkov, and most of the people active in RAPP, were in their family origins *petit-bourgeois* intellectuals. This was true not only of RAPP but also of the early On Guard group. Unlike the Proletcult,[1] whose tendency was to accept as proletarian only works directly expressing the life of the "labor collective," On Guard and RAPP had a much broader understanding of the term:

[1] "Proletcult": "Proletarian Culture," an organization of ultra-left intellectuals in the 1920's. [Editor's note.]

Proletarian literature we understand as that literature which comprehends the world from the viewpoint of the proletariat and influences the reader in accord with the tasks of the working class. . . . Only from the point of view of the world outlook of the proletariat — Marxism — can social reality be perceived by the artist with maximum objectivity.

Averbakh at one point clearly underlines the idea that the term "proletarian" has no necessary reference to the class origin of the writer:

Proletarian art is not a form of art which must necessarily be created by a proletarian. Proletarian art is such art as aids the proletariat in the building of socialism, and organizes our feelings and thoughts in the direction of the building of a communist society.

*   *   *

There emerged from this attempt to apply Marxism to literary theory and criticism a body of ideas some of which were not without objective merit. The emphasis on realism and against direct propaganda and obvious tendentiousness was the result of elementary lessons learned at the feet of Voronskii, and confirmed by the reading of Plekhanov.[2] The notion that reality is complex, unstable, and even a little mysterious, and that the "psyche" develops on more than one level and under influences not completely understood was an idea that the proletarians seem to have been groping for in their lengthy disquisitions on the "living man" and "immediate impressions." These ideas were of course woven into the fabric of "dialectical materialism," and the writer was required to portray reality from the viewpoint of the Marxist ideology. That this requirement did inhibit many writers, especially those in whom Marxism was not organic, could easily have been foreseen, and was in fact admitted by Averbakh and Libedinskii. If demanded mechanically of all writers its effect might be to discourage serious liter-

ary production. But as a viewpoint elected by a group of writers intent on exploring and perhaps explaining the world, it was capable of producing good results; and the proletarians did produce some works of genuine merit: we may mention Sholokhov's *The Silent Don*, Libedinskii's *Birth of a Hero*, Mitrofanov's *June-July*, and the early chapters of Panfërov's *Brusski*.

Yet there was a fatal flaw inherent in the nature of RAPP. The literary ideas of the leading group became articles of faith to which all writers within the organization were required to subscribe. The literary attitudes and habits of opposition groups were not granted autonomy. The fictitious and oppressive authority bestowed upon RAPP by the Party during these years tended to vitiate literary life, even within its own organization. Just how this happened we shall presently see. . . .

With the adoption of the first Five-Year Plan in 1928 the Party had undertaken a program which called for the maximum efforts in the direction of overcoming the industrial backwardness of the Soviet Union. Its program called for tremendous sacrifice and constant exertion. All forces were quite frankly "mobilized" for the task, and no exception was made for the forces of literature and art. Literary men, too, were expected to help in the colossal job of "overtaking and surpassing" the advanced countries; they were expected, in plain words, to devote their talents as writers to the humble task of publicizing and propagandizing the Plan. The idea that belles-lettres are an "instrument" in the hands of the dominant class — always the contention of the extreme left in Soviet theory — was now adopted by the Party in its simplest and crudest form.

With this change in the Party's attitude toward literature, the RAPP theory and practice began to lose favor; for the leaders of RAPP were slow, reluctant, and

[2] Alexander Voronskii, the leading Soviet literary critic of the 1920's; Georgi Plekhanov, the founder of Russian Marxism and a leader of the Mensheviks until his death in 1918. [Editor's note.]

ineffectual in carrying out the direct "social demand" of the Party. Under the pressure of its own program, the Party moved gradually but surely into a position of direct antagonism to the announced literary principles of RAPP, as set forth [above].

In the summer of 1928 the Central Committee of the Party called an all-Union conference on questions of agitation, propaganda, and cultural work. Among the resolutions adopted in the course of this discussion we find the following:

Literature, the theater, and the cinema should all be brought forward and into contact with the widest circles of the population, and should be utilized in the fight for a new cultural outlook, a new way of life, against bourgeois and *petit-bourgeois* ideology, against vodka, philistinism . . . against the resurrection of bourgeois ideology under new labels, and against a slavish imitation of bourgeois culture.

. . . [RAPP] was an organization made to order for the purposes of the Central Committee; it was composed mainly of Communists willing to undertake social tasks; it was organized and disciplined; it was already actively engaged in developing new writers from the working class; it announced as its chief virtue devotion in carrying out the policy of the Central Committee.

RAPP was the organization to which the Party would naturally turn as the chief support of its policy in the field of literary organization, literary production, and literary criticism. And while there is no statement of the Central Committee which definitely names RAPP as the spokesman of the Central Committee, yet it soon became clear that the Party depended upon RAPP to consolidate all Communist literary forces, to fight against "deviations" in the literary field, and to aid in carrying out literary directives. . . .

. . . A resolution of the Central Committee "On Publishing Work" was published on August 15, 1931. It lists the "successes" of Soviet publishing, pointing to the increase in number of titles issued, especially in the field of theory (the works of Lenin) and industrial technique. It goes on to point out what, in general, is expected of "the book":

The content and character of the book should in every way respond to the demands of socialist reconstruction; it should be militant and deal with political themes of the present day; it should arm the broad masses of the builders of socialism with Marxist-Leninist theory and with technical knowledge. The book should be the mightiest means of educating, mobilizing, and organizing the masses for the tasks of economic and cultural building.

Such is the Central Committee's description of what literature generally is expected to accomplish. On the subject of belles-lettres the resolution is no less definite as to the utilitarian aims to be pursued:

Imaginative literature, which plays such a huge educational role, should reflect far more deeply and fully the heroism of socialist construction and of the class struggle, the transformation of social relations and the growth of new people — the heroes of socialist construction. The publication of imaginative literature should be to a certain extent specialized by the GIKHL [State Publishing House for Belles-Lettres] into different sectors (for example, there should be, alongside synthetic imaginative works, historical literature, agricultural belles-lettres, industrial belles-lettres, classical literature, etc).

It should be clear that in the view of the Central Committee there was no question of eliminating entirely the production of literary works on historical subjects, or of such as are described as "synthetic," a term which apparently refers to fictional works having no immediate relation to the realities of socialist construction. It is clearly a question of emphasis. The Party policy is to increase the weight and relative importance of literature serving the ends of "socialist construction." And the Central Committee gave writers a material incentive for the production of such literature:

In view of the fact that the system of payment of authors has considerable importance in improving the quality of the printed work, it is necessary to differentiate payments, *and to set up such a scale of honorariums as will stimulate the promotion of the most talented authors; that is especially necessary in the case of those forms of literary production which have special importance for the present period.*

Thus it was the policy of the Central Committee in literature as in other sectors of "the economy" to use the incentive of higher pay in order to increase the production of "better quality" works, and by this they meant works answering the "needs of the day." It has not been possible to get reliable information on the scale of payments for literary works during this period; but it is reasonable to assume that more would be paid for a novel on the Dneprostroi construction than for a novel dealing with the "sufferings of mind" of an intellectual at odds with the epoch. It seems fairly certain on the basis of this official directive that there was, in fact, a wide differential in payments to authors, based in part on the importance of the subjects chosen in promoting the aims of "socialist reconstruction." This assumption is borne out, further, by the fact that Soviet writers generally gave themselves with a will to the depiction and stimulation of the labors of the Five-Year Plan. Thus the incentive of material success was added to the administrative directives, editorial propaganda, resolutions, and enterprises of the Central Committee, all aimed at producing a literature for and about the Five-Year Plan. In addition, there was undoubtedly present in many writers a genuine sympathy for the aims of the industrialization program and a real interest in the transformation of the country which was going on around them. . . .

The theory of proletarian literature dominant in RAPP was its most distinc-

tive and characteristic contribution to the movement. This theory was worked out in the heat of controversy with Proletcult and On Guard ideas on the left, and the views of Voronskii and the Pereval [3] critics on the right. In its final form it included elements of both. The theory described the nature of proletarian literature as cognition of life from the viewpoint of dialectical materialism, and its function as aiding the proletariat in its advance along the road to communism. It maintained that literature is an important instrument in the hands of the working class, and can be an effective means of changing reality, but only insofar as it deals directly with that reality itself. When it is unfaithful to reality — when it fails as "cognition of life" — then it is not literature and it is not an effective instrument. Proletarian literature must be realistic. It must continue the tradition of nineteenth-century Russian realism and accept as its cultural heritage the great masters of that school, particularly Tolstoy.

During the period of the first Five-Year Plan, this theory of literature and the practice based upon it came into conflict with the tremendous effort to rebuild the country which had been undertaken by the Party. In this effort the Party endeavored to enlist all forces, and its campaign affected every department of life. The psychology cultivated among the builders was essentially a military one, and the plan itself resembled a military campaign in its scale, its tempo, its slogans, and in the feeling of imminent war nourished by the Party. The urgent demand was to expend all energies so as to aid in fulfilling the goals of the plan. No exception was made for literature and the arts. Writers, too, had a function to perform, and literature was regarded as a means for mobilizing the masses. Thus under the pressure of its own program, the Party had adopted in its simplest form

[3] "Pereval": "The Pass," a group of politically moderate writers, forced out of existence around 1930. [Editor's note.]

the traditional viewpoint of the "left" in Soviet literary theory. It proposed to use literature as an instrument of its policy.

This development led to a curiously anomalous situation in which the organization supported by the Party and commissioned to mobilize proletarian forces on the literary front was out of harmony with the Party program for literature, both disapproving and resisting the effort to make literature an instrument of publicistic aims. Because of its leadership's lack of enthusiasm for carrying out Party directives, the organization was constantly torn by inner dissension, and heavily criticized from without by the Party press and Party spokesmen.

When RAPP was liquidated in April, 1932, many reasons were officially advanced for that step. The resolution of the Central Committee claims that a great growth in literature had taken place during the years of its activity, but concludes that RAPP should be liquidated. Kaganovich explained that liquidation was necessary because a few selfish Communists in RAPP had been "holding back the writers' creative powers." Party spokesmen in the years immediately following its dissolution gave a number of additional reasons for this step: the clannishness and isolation of the leading group, their administrative excesses, their theoretical deviations and "idealistic" alienation from the "Party spirit" of literature. All of these things may have been factors in the final decision.

The investigation undertaken here has produced evidence that there were two basic reasons for the dissolution of RAPP: its resistance to the Party's use of literature as an instrument of direct propaganda for the Five-Year Plan, and its hostility to a talented group of writers — the majority of them outside the Communist and proletarian milieu — of whose value to the Party as literary allies there was little doubt. It is suggested further that the dissolution of the proletarian literary organization was one indication of a decisive change in policy regarding the relative position and importance of the proletariat and other social groups. Thus ended the struggle for "proletarian hegemony," and all the discussions and disputes carried out in its name.

The period of the first Five-Year Plan was indeed a devastating one in the history of Russian literature. It marked the ruthless extension by the Communist Party of its political power into the field of belles-lettres. Russian literature has never recovered from that experience. RAPP was designed as an agency for the extension of Party power and as such it has occupied an unenviable place in literary history. Yet it must be remembered, to its credit, that at some time during this period Averbakh and the literary men associated with him discovered in themselves at least a modicum of care for the literature which others wished to use as an "instrument." Within the narrow limits of their class ideology — and they allowed themselves no other — they tried to save it.

The Crack down on the Party

NIKOLAI I. BUKHARIN

In 1936 the Russian Menshevik journal *Sotsialistichesky Vestnik* (The Socialist Messenger), then located in Paris, published a long letter from "a veteran member of the Bolshevik Party." It was actually written by the Menshevik historian Boris Nicolaevsky to record the substance of a series of talks that he had in Paris in the spring of 1936 with Nikolai Bukharin (1888–1938), leader of the ill-fated Right Opposition. The letter was translated into English and published in book form in 1938. In it Bukharin recounts the behind-the-scene maneuvering among the Soviet leadership in the early 1930's and the events leading up to the first of the "Moscow Trials" in 1936.

AMONG the last testaments left by Lenin there is none to which our "party leadership" had clung more tenaciously than his imperative advice not to repeat the mistake of the Jacobins — to eschew the road of mutual extermination. It was considered an axiom that in the fight against the Party Opposition any methods save the death penalty should be resorted to. True, there had been occasional lapses from this rule: *Blumkin* and a few other Trotskiites had been shot for penetrating, on instructions of their organization, into the secret recesses of the G.P.U., and warning their comrades against treachery and impending arrest. These shootings were generally regarded as exceptional measures, imposed not for participation in the struggle within the party, but for betrayal of official duties. Misdemeanours of this kind were always severely punished in the U.S.S.R. In 1924–1925 a Menshevik was shot who had forced his way into the secretariat of the Central Control Committee and had taken certain documents in order to send them to the *Socialist Messenger*. Even during the "Menshevik Trial" (1931) recourse to the death penalty had never been seriously considered.

The first occasion when the death penalty for participation in oppositionist activity in internal party politics was discussed was in connection with the Riutin affair. This was at the end of 1932, when the situation in the country was similar to 1921 — the time of the Kronstadt rebellion. In 1932, it is true, there were no actual revolts, but many believed that it would have been better if the Government had had to deal with actual revolts. Half of the country was stricken with famine. The workers were on short rations. The productivity of labour had greatly fallen, and there was no way of raising it, for it was not a question of unwillingness on the part of the workers, but of physical impossibility of working productively on an empty stomach. The predominant view in party circles was that Stalin had led the country into an impasse by his policy, that he had roused the peasants against the

From *Letter of an Old Bolshevik* (New York: The Rand School, and London: George Allen and Unwin, 1938), pp. 14–20, 22–25, 27–29, 69–71, 76. Reprinted by permission of George Allen and Unwin, Ltd. and of the Tamiment Institute of New York (successor to the Rand School).

party, and that the situation could be saved only by his removal from party domination. Many influential members of the Central Committee were of this opinion. It was said that an anti-Stalin majority was being formed in the "Politburo" as well. Wherever party officials met, the subject of discussion was: what programme was to be substituted for Stalin's "general line." It is obvious that, in the process, various proposed programmes and declarations were being circulated from hand to hand. Among these, Riutin's programme was specially noteworthy. It was definitely pro-peasant in character. It demanded the abolition of the collectives and the granting of economic self-determination to the peasants. But this was not all that differentiated this programme from others. At that time the programme of the right-wing Bolsheviks, such as that of Slepkov, was emphatically pro-peasant, but so was that of the former left-wing Trotskiists, who had been, in fact, politically responsible for Stalin's "general line," since it was they who had been its original ideologists. Riutin's programme was remarkable chiefly for its *severe criticism of Stalin*. It was two hundred pages long, fifty of which were devoted to Stalin's personal characteristics, to a consideration of the part he had played in the party, and to the reasons for the basic contention that unless Stalin was removed from party domination there could be no recovery in the party or in the country. These views were expressed with remarkable vigour and made a deep impression. Stalin was depicted as the evil genius of the Russian Revolution, who, actuated by vindictiveness and lust for power, had brought the revolution to the edge of the abyss.

This section of the programme, for which the author was to pay a heavy penalty, was particularly responsible for its success. The programme aroused a great deal of discussion, and it was not surprising, therefore, that a copy was soon brought to Stalin's desk. This, naturally,

led to arrests and house-searches. As a result, not only were all those who had circulated Riutin's programme arrested, but also those who had distributed other declarations. Riutin, who at that time was in exile or in an "isolator," where he had worked out his plan, was brought to Moscow. Upon examination, he admitted the authorship. As an old party leader who had rendered eminent service to the party, he came within the classification of those against whom, in accordance with Lenin's commandment, there could be no question of application of the death penalty. The question was, therefore, considered by the "Politburo," because the O.G.P.U. (naturally, at Stalin's wish) had demanded his execution.

The discussions in the "Politburo" were heated. Stalin was in favour of granting the O.G.P.U.'s demand. His strongest argument was a reference to the growth of *terrorist sentiment among young people,* particularly in the Komsomol (Young Communist League). Reports of the O.G.P.U. were replete with stories of terroristic talk among *young workers and students.* Moreover, quite a number of terroristic acts against minor Soviet Officials and party officers had become known. Against such terrorists the party did not shrink from resorting to the "supreme penalty," even when it was a question of members of the Komsomol, Stalin maintaining that it was politically illogical and unjust to administer such severe punishment to those who performed terroristic acts while sparing those whose political propaganda had inspired these acts. He recommended that no undue attention be given to the small fry, but that the "Politburo" go straight to the root and cause of the matter. Riutin's programme, Stalin said, was a direct justification of and an apology for the necessity of murdering him.

I can no longer recall the actual division of opinion in the "Politburo" when this question was being considered. I only know that Kirov[1] spoke with particular force against recourse to the death penalty. Moreover, he succeeded in winning over the "Politburo" to this view. Stalin was prudent enough not to push matters to an open conflict. Riutin's life was thus spared. He was sentenced to a long term in an "isolator" where a particularly severe regime was in vogue. It became clear to everybody, however, that the "Politburo" would be compelled again to take up the big questions which had arisen, in one form or another, out of this affair. . . .

Kirov played an important part in the "Politburo." He was a one hundred per cent supporter of the "general line," and distinguished himself during its operation by great energy and inflexibility. This caused Stalin to value him highly. But there was always a certain independence in Kirov's attitude which annoyed Stalin. The story is told that Stalin had prevented Kirov from attending the meetings of the "Politburo" in Moscow for several months under the pretext that his presence in Leningrad was indispensable. However, Stalin could never make up his mind to take strong measures against Kirov. It would have been folly to add to the already large number of the dissatisfied an important party leader such as Kirov, especially since Kirov had succeeded in surrounding himself in Leningrad with reliable and devoted aids. A new conflict with the Leningrad party might have been more fatal now than in Zinoviev's day. In the winter of 1933–34, Kirov had so strengthened his position that he could afford to follow his own line. He aimed not only at a "Western orientation" in foreign policy, but also at the conclusions which would follow logically from this new orientation as far as home policy was concerned.

The task, therefore, was not only that of creating a mighty army in preparation for the impending military conflict, a conflict which appeared inevitable, but also, politically speaking, of creating the proper psychologic frame of mind on the home front. There were two alternatives: to pursue the former policy of crushing all dissenters, with the administrative pressure ruthlessly tightened and the terror intensified, or to try "reconciliation with the people," to gain their voluntary cooperation in the political preparation of the country for the coming war. The most convinced and most prominent advocates of the *second alternative* were *Kirov* and *Gorki* [Maxim Gorki, the writer]. It would be worth while to describe in greater detail Gorki's influence in the life of the party, particularly as it is now possible to speak more openly since his death. But that is another matter, and would take us too far afield. Gorki had exercised a great and beneficent influence upon Stalin. But, despite all his influence, Gorki was *not a member* of the "Politburo," and had no direct part in the making of its decisions. Kirov's part became, therefore, all the more important.

Kirov stood for the idea of *abolition of the terror*, both in general and inside the party. We do not desire to exaggerate the importance of his proposals. It must not be forgotten that when the first Five-Year Plan was being put into effect, Kirov was one of the heads of the party, that he was among those who inspired and carried through the notoriously ruthless measures against the peasants and the wiping out of the kulaks. The Kem and Murmansk coasts, with their prison camps, etc., were under his jurisdiction. Furthermore, he was in charge of the construction of the Baltic-White Sea Canal. This is enough to make it clear that Kirov could not be reproached with any undue tenderness in the manner in which he disposed of human lives. But this very fact added to his strength in the official circles in which he had to defend his point of view. That he had so large a share of responsibility

[1] Sergei M. Kirov, member of the Politburo, First Secretary of the Communist Party for the Leningrad Province, and Stalin's apparent second-in-command until his assassination under mysterious circumstances in December, 1934. [Editor's note.]

in the horrors of the first Five-Year Plan made it possible for him to come forward as a leader and protagonist of the policy of moderating the terror during the second Five-Year Plan. Kirov's line of thought ran as follows: The period of destruction, which was necessary to extirpate the small proprietor elements in the villages, was now at an end; the economic position of the collectives was consolidated and made secure for the future. This constituted a firm basis for future development, and as the economic situation continued to improve, the broad masses of the population would become more and more reconciled to the government; the number of "internal foes" would diminish. It was now the task of the party to rally those forces which would support it in the new phase of economic development, and thus to broaden the foundation upon which Soviet power was based. Kirov, therefore, strongly advocated reconciliation with those party elements who, during the period of the first Five-Year Plan, had gone over to the Opposition, but who might be induced to co-operate on the new basis, now that the "destructive" phase was over. . . .

. . . Early in the summer of 1933, when it became certain that the harvest would be good, Kamenev, Zinoviev and a number of other former members of the Opposition were once again re-admitted as members of the party. They were even permitted to choose their spheres of work, and some of them actually received invitations to the party congress (February 1934).

At that congress Kirov appeared in triumph. Previously, his election in Leningrad had been celebrated as was no other. At district conferences in various parts of the city, all of which he toured on the same day, he had been received with wild cheers. "Long live our Mironitch!" the delegates shouted; it had been an exceedingly impressive demonstration and it showed that the entire Leningrad proletariat was behind Kirov. At the party

congress, too, Kirov received an extraordinarily enthusiastic reception. He was cheered, the entire assembly rising to its feet on hearing his report. During the recesses there was discussion as to who had had the more tumultuous reception, Kirov or Stalin. This very comparison shows how strong Kirov's influence had already become.

Not only was Kirov re-elected to the "Politburo," but he was also chosen a secretary of the Central Committee, making it necessary for him to move to Moscow within a short time to take over direction of a whole group of departments which had heretofore been under *Postichev* and *Kaganovitch*. This was to insure putting into effect the new line which Kirov had inspired. His removal to Moscow was delayed, however. The official reason given was that his presence in Leningrad was indispensable; a substitute was supposedly being sought in Leningrad, but until someone could be found fit to take his place, his transfer to Moscow had to be postponed. In spite of this, he took part in the work of the "Politburo," and his influence there continued to grow. . . .

. . . [Kirov's assassination put an end to any chance for liberation within the party. Thereafter] the trend was in quite the opposite direction: not toward reconciliation inside the party, but toward intensification of the terror inside the party to its logical conclusion, to the stage of *physical extermination of all those whose party past might make them opponents of Stalin or aspirants to his power*. To-day, I have not the slightest doubt that it was at that very period, between the murder of Kirov and the second Kamenev trial, that Stalin made his decision and mapped out his plan of "reforms," an essential component part of which was the trial of the *sixteen* and *other trials yet to come*. If, before the murder of Kirov, Stalin still had some hesitation as to which road to choose, he had now made up his mind.

The determining reason for Stalin's decision was his realization, arrived at on the basis of reports and information reaching him, that *the mood of the majority of the old party workers was really one of bitterness and hostility toward him.*

The trials and investigations which followed the Kirov affair had demonstrated unmistakably that the party had not reconciled itself to Stalin's personal dictatorship; that, in spite of all their solemn declarations, the old Bolsheviks rejected Stalin in the depths of their hearts, that this attitude of hostility, instead of diminishing, was growing, and that the majority of those who cringed before him, protesting devotion, would betray him at the first change of the political atmosphere.

This was the basic fact that emerged for Stalin from the documents compiled in the course of the investigation of Nikolaiev's act [the assassination of Kirov]. It must be conceded that Stalin was able to provide a reasonable basis for this deduction, and from it he fearlessly drew his ultimate conclusions. As Stalin perceived it, the reasons for the hostility toward him lay in *the basic psychology of the old Bolsheviks.* Having grown up under the conditions of revolutionary struggle against the old regime, we had all been trained in the psychology of oppositionists, of irreconcilable non-conformists. Involuntarily, our minds work in a direction *critical* of the existing order; we seek everywhere its weak sides. In short, we are all critics, destructionists — not builders. This was all to the good — in the past; but now, when we must occupy ourselves with constructive building, it is all hopelessly bad. It is impossible to build anything enduring with such human materials, composed of sceptics and critics. What must be considered now, first and foremost, is the necessity of enduring Soviet construc-

tion, particularly because Soviet Russia is facing tremendous perturbations, such as will arise inevitably with the coming of war. It was thus that Stalin reasoned.

The conclusion he drew from all this was certainly daring: if the old Bolsheviks, the group constituting to-day the ruling caste in the country, are unfit to perform this function, it is necessary to remove them from their posts, to create *a new ruling caste. Kirov's* plans presupposed reconciliation with the non-party intelligentsia and enlistment of non-party workers and peasants in the tasks of social and political life, as a means of widening the social basis of the Soviet regime and promoting its co-operation with the democratic elements of the population. Under *Stalin's* plan these very same proposals acquired quite a different significance; they were to facilitate a complete revision of the personnel of the ruling caste by expelling from its midst all those infected with the spirit of criticism, and the substitution of a new ruling caste, governed by a new psychology aiming at positive construction. . . .

All of us old *Bolsheviks* who have any sort of prominent revolutionary past are now hiding in our lairs, trembling. For has it not been demonstrated theoretically that under present circumstances we are an undesirable element? It is sufficient for any one to have crossed the path of a person implicated in an investigation for his fate to be sealed. No one will dare defend us. At the same time, all sorts of "benefits" and "alleviations" are being heaped upon the general population. The purpose of this is deliberate: let the memory of our crucifixion be inextricably bound in the minds of the people with the "improvements" they have received from Stalin.

IV. EVALUATIONS AND EXPLANATIONS

The Logic of Russian History

WALTER DURANTY

Walter Duranty (1884–1957) was the Moscow Correspondent of the New York Times from 1921 to 1933. His dispatches have been collected and published in several books, including Russia Reported. The selections which appear here are from dispatches which Duranty wrote from Paris in the summer of 1931. There he was free from the Soviet censorship and able to comment without restraint on the historical meaning of the events of the Stalin Revolution which he had been witnessing.

PARIS, *June 13, 1931.* — Russia to-day cannot be judged by Western standards or interpreted in Western terms. Western Marxists and socialists go nearly as far wrong about it as the "bourgeois" critics because they fail to understand that the dominant principle of the Soviet Union, though called Marxism or communism, is now a very different thing from the theoretical conception advanced by Karl Marx.

In thirteen years Russia has transformed Marxism — which was only a theory anyway — to suit its racial needs and characteristics, which are strange and peculiar, and fundamentally more Asiatic than European.

The dominant principle in Russia to-day is not Marxism or even Leninism, although the latter is its official title, but Stalinism — to use a word which Joseph Stalin deprecates and rejects. I mean that, just as Leninism meant Marxian theory plus practical application plus Russia, so Stalinism denotes a further development from Leninism and bears witness to the prodigious influence of the Russian character and folkways upon what seemed the rigid theory of Marx.

Stalinism is a tree that has grown from the alien seed of Marxism planted in Russian soil, and whether Western communists like it or not it is a Russian tree.

Old Russia was an amorphous mass, held together by a mystic, half-Asiatic idea of an imperial regime wherein the emperor was exalted to the position of God's viceregent, with limitless power over the bodies, souls, property, and even thoughts of his subjects. That, at least, was the theory, and it was only when the Tsars themselves began to question it and "act human" that a spirit of doubt and eventual rebellion became manifest.

The Tsarist regime was poisoned by the European veneer that was spread over Russia — a veneer that was foreign and at bottom unwelcome to the mass of the Russian people — and one of the things the Bolshevik revolution did was to sweep away this alien crust and give the essential Russianism underneath an opportunity to

From *Duranty Reports Russia* by Walter Duranty (British edition entitled *Russia Reported*), selected and arranged by Gustavus Tuckerman, Jr. Copyright each year 1921–1933 by the New York Times; 1934 by Walter Duranty (New York: The Viking Press; London: Victor Gollancz, 1934), pp. 237–241, 266–268. Reprinted by permission of the Viking Press, Inc., and of Curtis Brown Ltd.

breathe and grow. Which explains why the Bolsheviki, who at first were a mere handful among Russia's millions, were able successfully to impose their dominant principle — namely, Marxism — which in superficial appearance was far more alien than the Germanised or Westernised system it overthrew.

The truth is that the ideas outlined in the *Communist Manifesto* of Marx (which incidentally expounds his whole philosophy far more simply, lucidly, and concretely than the ponderous *Kapital* and should be learned by heart by anyone who wishes to understand the Soviet Union) suited the Russian masses much better then the Western theory of individualism and private enterprise imported by Peter the Great and his successors, who finally perished in the conflict it involved with the native character of Russia.

Lenin took and shaped Marxism to fit the Russian foot and, although circumstances compelled him to abandon it temporarily for the New Economic Policy, he always maintained that this political manœuvre was not a basic change of policy. Sure enough, Stalin, his successor and devout disciple, first emasculated Nep and then set about abolishing it. To-day Nep is a sorry slave in the outer courts of the Soviet palace.

That is what Stalin did and is doing to our boasted Western individualism and spirit of personal initiative — which was what Nep meant — not because Stalin is so powerful or cruel and full of hate for the capitalist system as such, but because he has an unrivalled genius for political management since Charles Murphy died.

Stalin is giving the Russian people — the Russian masses, not Westernised landlords, industrialists, bankers, and intellectuals, but Russia's 150,000,000 peasants and workers — what they really want, namely, joint effort, communal effort; and communal life is as acceptable to them as it is repugnant to a Westerner. This is one of the reasons why Russian Bolshevism will never succeed in the United States, Great Britain, France, or other parts west of the Rhine.

Stalinism, too, has done what Lenin only attempted. It has re-established the semi-divine, supreme autocracy of the imperial idea and has placed itself on the Kremlin throne as a ruler whose lightest word is all in all and whose frown spells death. Try that on free-born Americans, or the British with their tough loyalty to old things, or on France's consciousness of self. But it suits the Russians and is as familiar, natural, and right to the Russian mind as it is abominable and wrong to Western nations.

This Stalin knows, and that knowledge is his key to power. Stalin does not think of himself as a dictator or an autocrat, but as the guardian of the sacred flame, or "party line," as the Bolsheviki term it, which for want of a better name must be labelled Stalinism.

Its authority is as absolute as any emperor's — it is an inflexible rule of thought, ethics, conduct, and purpose that none may transgress. And its practical expression finds form in what is known as the Five-Year Plan. The Soviet Five-Year Plan is a practical expression of the dominant principle — which for convenience the writer will call Stalinism, although Stalin still terms it Leninism — that rules Russia to-day with absolute authority.

In a sense it far more than a plan — and in another sense it is not a plan at all. It is a slogan for a national policy and purpose rather than the glorified budgetary programme which it appears at first sight to be. Most persons outside Russia seem to think that, if the Five-Year Plan "fails," it will be the end of Bolshevism and that, if it "succeeds," it will mean the end of capitalism elsewhere. Nothing could be more absurd or more wrong.

The Five-Year Plan is nothing more or less than applied Stalinism, and its mass of bewildering figures is only the thermometer to measure the degree of heat engendered by the application of the plan, but is not otherwise intrinsically important.

The figures have been changed so often and so considerably as to cease to have real value save as an indication of the "tempo," or rate, at which Stalinism is gaining ground.

To the rest of the world it is a menace only in the sense that Bolshevism itself is a menace — which may or may not be true. To Russia it is only a hope or promise in terms of what Bolshevism itself offers. But to the Russian people the Five-Year Plan is infinitely more besides — it is a goal to aim at, and its inception cannot but be regarded as a stroke of genius by anyone familiar with the Russian nature.

Russians, ignorant or wise, have a positive passion for plans. They almost worship a plan, and the first thing any one, two, or more Russians ever do about anything is to make a plan for it. That, after making his plan, the Russian feels satisfied and seems to lose sight of the fact that a plan must next be carried out is one of the great obstacles Stalin and his associates are now facing.

So, to conceive a whole national policy and everything in the national life as one gigantic plan was the political *tour de force* that put Stalin in the highest rank. Everyone who has employed Russians or worked with Russians or knows Russians finds that, if he wants them to jump on a chair, he must tell them to jump on a table, and aiming at the table they will reach the chair. The important thing is that they have something to jump at and make an effort — whether they actually get there at once or not does not really matter in a country of such vast natural resources and with such a tough and enduring population.

What matters is that they keep on trying, and that is what Stalinism and its Five-Year Plan is set to make them do. In other words, the Five-Year Plan is something for the Russians to measure at, not for the rest of the world to measure Russians by. This sounds confusing, but it is true, and if you cannot understand it you cannot understand Russia. . . .

PARIS, *June 27, 1931.* — The characteristic of Stalinism that marks the continuing curve of progress from alien Marxism through semi-alien, semi-Russian Leninism toward something not yet attained, is that Russian Stalinism still is stiffening Communist party discipline.

This discipline is modified, as shown in a previous dispatch, by "self-criticism," but is centralised and administered with military rigidity. No excuse or evasion of party orders is permitted, and infractions of discipline are punished by a reprimand, or, if repeated, by expulsion from the party.

Of this, Joseph Stalin himself, only five years ago, speaking in behalf of Leon Trotsky, when Leonid Kamenev and Gregory Zinoviev urged his expulsion, said:

"Expulsion is a final and fatal weapon to be employed only in a hopeless case."

To-day party members, even the highest placed — or the lowest placed and youngest, which is perhaps even more important — must give full obedience or take the consequences. Much water has run under Bolshevik bridges since December 1925, and profoundly have time and circumstances modified earlier conceptions.

Marxism was a theory, clear-cut enough in its fundamentals — which, be it always remembered, Stalinism retains almost without amendment — but necessarily vague as to practice and application.

Leninism — anyway, at the outset, as the records show — was a sort of debating society where a small group of devoted comrades discussed policies with freedom and equality, sometimes wasting time and energy in discussion.

Stalinism is an imperial sceptre, not decked with the golden orb and cross and the Orlov diamond of Tsarist rule but a bar of polished steel.

Stalin's opponents accuse him of absolutism, and it is true and false. Absolutism there is — not that Stalin wants it for his ambition or vainglory but because the circumstances and Russia demand it; because there is no more time for argument or discussion or even freedom in the Western sense, for which Russia cares nothing, because, in short, a house divided against itself cannot stand in an hour of stress.

Outsiders may write nonsense about Stalin's egoism and the purely personal quality of "the struggle for power" between him and Trotsky or Alexei Rykov or Zinoviev. Personal elements do and must enter into all human relations, but in default of familiarity with the New Russia these critics might study the early history of the Christian church, which was racked and torn far worse by "ideological controversy," as the Bolsheviki call it, than by the rivalries of leaders which came after the councils of Nicæa "set" or crystallised doctrinal confusion.

The parallel is sharper and closer than either Christians or Bolsheviki would care to admit. Christianity was a product of transcendent Jewish idealism, aimed at redressing inequality between man and man and establishing true human brotherhood and happiness. Marxism also.

The Roman Emperor Constantine made Christianity the state religion under an absolute ruler whose attitude toward what had been a persecuted and almost "revolutionary" creed was wholly changed. Lenin made Marxism the state religion of Russia, with a change no less inevitable.

Christianity was further transmuted by contact with the Nordic nations of Europe, by their adaptation of it to suit their separate "Volkgeist" [national spirit]. So now Russia, with its ancient Asiatic craving for mass action under an absolute ruler whose word is the law and the prophets, changes Marxism further into something grim and Russian over which orthodox Marxists abroad wring their hands and the Western world cries "slavery and terror."

The Logic of the Revolution

RUDOLF SCHLESINGER

Rudolf Schlesinger (1909–1961) was a German-English scholar of Marxist persuasion who wrote extensively on Soviet doctrine and social policies. In The Spirit of Post-War Russia he sketched a history of how Soviet thinking and aims had evolved since the Revolution. He took the unusual view that the Stalin Revolution was a breakaway from the original Marxist plan, but that it was nevertheless necessary and desirable to bring the Russian Revolution to complete fruition.

THE Russia of the NEP, that the British Trade Unionist Delegation visited in 1925 . . . , made a strong impression not only on them, but on progressive minds in the West in general. For it was still very near to the average Western progressive mentality. Its economics were run along easily comprehensible lines, with a larger number of factories in public ownership than any Western Socialist dared to dream of for another generation. This country, the most backward in Europe only ten years previously, now had the most progressive labour legislation.

From Rudolf Schlesinger, *The Spirit of Post-War Russia* (London: Dennis Dobson, Ltd., 1947), pp. 13–19. Reprinted by permission of the publisher.

Even if there were some unemployment— and of course there was if the State itself had to close down its factories when working uneconomically — the treatment of the unemployed was more liberal than in any other country. There were the most powerful trade unions in the world, with an acknowledged share in the government of state-owned factories, but also with the right to strike occasionally (especially, of course, in the privately-owned factories). No judge or policeman interfered with such strikes. Last but not least there was quite a remarkable amount of freedom even of public political discussion. It is true, with a few recognized exceptions, this was restricted to the factions of the one ruling party, and the opinions discussed had to be expressed in a certain political jargon. But it does not much matter what a thing is called. Eager prophets might foretell the transformation of these factions into several parties representing, within a virtually parliamentary regime, the interests of the various strata of the population. Certain ideological limits were set for the members of the ruling party but, apart from this, the Russia of the NEP was anything but a totalitarian state. Anyone who sincerely believed that the Tsar and the landlords had been dealt with according to their deserts, and that the Church should deal only with spiritual affairs, enjoyed a quite remarkable freedom of expression.

Had the Revolution been able to stop short at this point the Bolsheviks would have achieved, with due modifications for twentieth-century conditions such as the nationalization of the big factories, banks, etc., what the Jacobins had attempted. Backward Russia would have become the most advanced democratic country in the sense of the French Revolution and of the Chartist Movement.[1] In due course out of the well-to-do farmers, and successful merchants, a new middle class would have

developed. The enthusiasts for the new state of affairs, like Bukharin, might hope that this class would "automatically," by the progress of co-operation, "grow into Socialism." The more sceptical might call the same process a transformation of the Soviet Republic into an "ordinary" liberal though doubtless a very progressive state with the most advanced social legislation, the most progressive schools and by far the most advanced nationality policies in the world. Doubtless it would have been worth the millions of victims fallen in the great struggle. Russia, even so, would have entered the ranks of the leading nations of the world. He who dreamed of the former Socialist ideals might rest assured that the workers of the West as well as the colonial slaves of the East would have received a clear lesson that revolution does pay. Russia would have done her part — provided only she could stay where she was. But she could not.

Without capitalists, but with the most progressive labour legislation in the world, the state-owned factories worked better than they had done in private hands. Within a few years they reached and surpassed the pre-war level. But how, under these conditions of labour, could sufficient profits be made to build new factories at more than a very modest pace? The well-to-do peasants were highly satisfied with the freedom of trade. But they took it to mean that they were allowed to retain the bulk of the harvest until late in spring and then to use the shortness of supply as an instrument of pressure to extort economic and political concessions. The "tax in natura"[2] prevented the worst. But year by year spring was announced by a political crisis within the ruling party, caused essentially by the problem of what concessions to grant the kulaks (well-to-do farmers). And the richer they grew, the more they asked. In the spring of 1928 things came very near to a strike of supply. The

[1] The Chartist Movement: British democratic movement of the 1830's and 1840's. [Editor's note.]

[2] "Tax in natura": The "tax in kind," a limited tax on the peasants which replaced the unlimited "requisitioning" of food in 1921. [Editor's note.]

state had to answer by measures that left nothing of the principle of free trade but the name. What would the peasants do in the case of war?

And war would come — maybe war against a united capitalist world. So the Russians thought, as anyone who was in their country then will admit, at least since 1927 when the Tory government followed Locarno with the rupture of Anglo-Russian diplomatic relations. This conviction of the responsible leaders of Russian policy decided the whole pace of subsequent events. I am, consciously, speaking merely of the pace. In no case could revolutionary Russia have allowed herself to be starved, or brought under political pressure, by the kulaks. And even the most modest aspirations for her future reconstruction needed a greater degree of industrialization than could be obtained without greater efforts. But a different pace in Soviet industrialization and collectivization, if it had been possible without risking the defeat of the Revolution, would have meant the whole difference between some additional economic exertion and the enormous price in human suffering and spiritual sacrifice that the Russian Revolution was to pay for its survival. Had external peace been secured, the grain stocks accumulated as a war reserve together with the normal activities of the tax-collector should have sufficed to bring the kulak to reason. In due course home-built or imported agricultural machines would have made it possible for the co-operative to throw him out of the market by "peaceful" competition. And had it been possible freely to import foreign machines and to concentrate on building the factories necessary for a peaceful economic development, industrialization would hardly have cost the country more than the postponement of some otherwise desirable wage-increases or social reforms. There would then have been no danger of dissent growing within the Party to such a degree that the "outs" accused the "ins" of betraying the Revolution, and that the "ins" believed (and had

moreover good reason to believe) that such propaganda by the "outs" might bring about the downfall of the revolutionary régime. I doubt very much whether there is much chance of finding *in Moscow* the individuals responsible (in so far as individuals have some responsibility for great historical events) for the fact that tens of thousands of kulaks were to die in the northern forests, that the freedom of the churches was to be reduced to mere worship while all religious propaganda was forbidden, and that dissent within the Party on essentials of politics was to be regarded as a kind of treason. Whoever in Berlin, since 1918, was responsible for a policy that demanded Western capitalist support for defeating the German revolution, based on the promise that bourgeois Germany would form a bulwark of Western civilization against the Bolshevist danger, whoever in London, in the spring of 1927, was responsible for the Arcos[3] raid, inevitably succeeded in convincing the Russians that they had, at any price, to prepare for war. You can, of course, accuse them of having partly been frightened by a nightmare, for neither Baldwin nor Chamberlain brought Britain into war against the U.S.S.R. Nevertheless they made it possible for someone else to wage war against the U.S.S.R. as well as against Britain. In view of recent events one can hardly deny the full justification of every sacrifice that enabled the U.S.S.R., by industrialization and agricultural collectivization, to be prepared for the ordeal.

Full preparedness for an approaching war once given as a condition for the survival of revolutionary Russia, events had to take their course: what in fact was a second revolution (as the Russians now acknowledge) had become inevitable. If grain was to be collected by force from the kulak he was bound to sabotage production. The state, therefore, was bound not only to arrest the kulak, but to replace

[3] "Arcos": The Anglo-Russian Trading Co., a Soviet agency in London, raided by the police in 1927 on suspicion of espionage. [Editor's note.]

him, since the country could not exist without grain. The kulak was to be replaced by agricultural co-operatives which would, at first, be supported only by the poor peasants who immediately gained by the expropriation of the kulak. For the experiment had to be made before there was anything like a sufficient amount of agricultural machinery to make these co-operatives, the kollkhoses, a convincing success from the point of view of the average peasant. Lacking conviction that collectivization meant prosperity for him, the peasant, when induced to join the kollkhoses would, in most cases, previously slaughter his cattle. There would be shortage of food and rationing in the towns. The state would have to build a considerable number of factories which, by the very nature of armament production, were bound to devour a large part of the national income without at any time refunding the labour involved in their construction in the shape of goods increasing the national wealth. Another large group of factories in the heavy industries would make that contribution, by producing useful goods for peacetime industries, only many years after their construction had devoured billions of roubles. Imports of foreign machinery would be necessary. These imports would not only have to replace the valuable consumption goods which could otherwise have been imported — to pay for them it would even be necessary to export some of the butter which the urban population needed. Certainly, during the first years, less rather than more food would be available. But millions of people would enter industry to build new factories, some under inconceivably hard conditions. These new millions of workers would have to share with the millions already employed in industry a rather limited supply of goods suitable for individual consumption.

In compensation for all their exertions the state could, in the beginning, give its citizens little but the conviction that they were building the material foundations of a new and better society. The state, there-

fore, had to oppose by every means those who denied the possibility of building, in contemporary Russia, such a society. The latter were bound, by their very convictions, to oppose with all available means what, in their eyes, must seem to be a senseless exploitation of the people by leaders who had betrayed the Revolution. What was growing in the Russia of the late 'twenties and early 'thirties was bound to appear, in the eyes of the opponents, to be merely a kind of state-capitalism which every class-conscious worker was bound to oppose by the usual methods of a radical labour movement. But a state which, in its very struggle for survival, was bound daily to do in a hundred places things that, under normal conditions, would undoubtedly justify the workers in calling a strike, was bound to consider as enemies of the Revolution people who spoke of "state-capitalism" and, thus, were likely to organise strikes against socialist reconstruction. From the point of view of the opposition, Stalin's state was counter-revolutionary; it was a specially dangerous kind of counter-revolution because it was able to deceive the workers by revolutionary phraseology. Against such an adversary any method of struggle, including the preparation of armed force, seemed justified from the Trotskyist point of view. There are certain fundamental Communist views on the tactics to be applied once a reactionary state is confronted with external war. Karl Liebknecht[4] had taught that it is in each Socialist's own country that he has to look for the enemy. For the Trotskyist the enemy was in Russia.

Thus all the tragedy of the later purges was made inevitable by the developments of 1929–33. Millions, many more than had participated in the battles of the Civil War, paid the heaviest sacrifices for what they believed the future of their people in "peaceful" work in icy steppes or in the everyday struggle with the dark inheritance

[4] Karl Liebknecht: Leader of the left wing of the German Socialists at the time of World War I. [Editor's note.]

of the Russian village. But in the same fateful years thousands of people who had shared in the first struggle despairingly doubted whether it had been worth while to fight for such a future.

Much later on, when all was over, Stalin wrote a very characteristic passage, expressing something that, during those years, everyone had known, but hardly anyone had dared to express openly. The collectivization of agriculture had been "a profound revolution . . . equivalent in its consequences to the revolution of October 1917. The distinguishing feature of this revolution is that it was accomplished *from above*, on the initiative of the state, and directly *supported from below*" — by the peasants participating in the anti-kulak and collectivization movements.

It is somewhat surprising that none, so far as I can remember, of the many writers on Russian problems has appreciated the whole importance in the evolution of Soviet ideology of this acknowledgement. "Revolution from above" had, hitherto, not been exactly popular with Marxist opinion, including opinion in Russia. There is, of course, an enormous difference between a "revolution from above" initiated by a state intent on securing and developing the achievements of the "revolution from below" which had created it only ten years before and, on the other hand, that "revolution from above" by which Bismarck took the wind out of the sails of the 1848 "revolutionaries from below." And it is the latter instance that forms the basis of most Marxian opinion on "revolution from above." But the left-wing everywhere is in the habit of glorifying the revolutionary initiative of the masses as distinct from state authority. During the great crisis, the Russians themselves were no exception to this rule, as anyone who has seen a film or read a Soviet book on the events of the First Five-Year Plan will confirm. The heroes are the workers of the factory who answer the cautious and hesitant plans of old-fashioned specialists with "counter-plans" and suc-ceed against all the handicaps imposed by red tape in realizing these plans; or the poor young peasants who against all the prejudices of their neighbours, including the local or district organs of the Party, succeed in building a flourishing kollkhos. The leaders of party and state are kept rather in the background, directing the revolutionary efforts from below as Lenin had, from his hiding place, directed the exertions of the 1917 revolutionaries. Without undue violence to the facts one can, in either case, stress one side or the other of the picture — the rôle of the leaders or the rôle of the masses. When speaking, in 1938, of the 1928–33 revolution Stalin preferred to stress not only the rôle of the leaders, as the Bolsheviks had always done, but also particularly the fact that they had acted as leaders of the state; all achievements of the Revolution now at last firmly established were due to the state. Evidently the latter was not, as Lenin had thought all his life, the mere ephemeral instrument of the victorious working classes, destined to "wither away" and to make room for a free community based on personal freedom and voluntary subordination to the will of the majority. Utopia had, in 1938, fallen back before reality. The Revolution was accomplished.

Just as during the first great crisis of the Revolution, in the period of "War-Communism," so also during the second, the rapid industrialization of the country and collectivization of agriculture, there were people who attempted to make a revolutionary programme out of the necessities of the hour. The leftist saw that the old specialists and the right-wingers of the Party could not imagine Russia as a first-class industrial country and deemed it impossible to build huge modern factories out of almost nothing. The leftist had to fight such an attitude; therefore, to him, the giant scale of an economic project seemed in itself, independent of its economic merits, an achievement for Socialism. To build more and still more new giant factories came to be regarded as an essential element of future progress, as opposed to the capitalist countries where, during the great depression, harvests were being ploughed in and factory-plants were being destroyed.

In the young and poor kollkhoses, enthusiasm had to replace economic rewards for increased exertions, and even in industry the stimulating effects of piece-work were problematic when the only part of the national income accessible to the worker was the minimum granted on the ration-books. The most secure way of distributing extra food among the people doing heavy work, without risking the goods going on the black market to the highest bidder, was to organize canteens providing cheap meals in the factories. And the necessary condition for drawing young peasant women into industrial work or even into work in the kollkhos was to organize crèches for their infants. All these things found sufficient justification in the facts of everyday life. But Soviet ideology during the First Five-Year Plan tended to build out of such natural facts of actual organization a conception of the coming socialist society without any private interests and private life at all. If possible even the pullets in the kollkhos had to be collectivized. Any personal care of the parents for their children was regarded as very nearly a reactionary prejudice. The community had to fill not only a very important part — as any Soviet people would agree — but nearly the whole, or at the least the central place in any citizen's mind, and the interest of the community had to replace such inferior stimuli as private interest. In fact, the Dnieper aggregate, Magnitogorsk and Kusnjetzk arose, out of the steppes, and 200,000 kollkhoses were organized, out of a semi-illiterate peasantry, without the people who accomplished these things expecting any other reward than the consciousness of having helped to build a better life for the community. Such inspiration, in war as well as in revolution, is the great strength of the Soviet peoples. But could they be expected to build an effi-

cient national economy for everyday purposes on such lines?

The responsible leaders of the Soviet state did not believe in ideologies as a sufficient basis for permanent social organization, nor in the permanent efficiency of mere enthusiasm as a stimulus for the average man and woman. One could not proceed indefinitely in the spirit of the First Five-Year Plan. Besides, would it be worth while? The threat of war had stood behind the plan, and this spectre now put on flesh and blood. Whilst the new factories arose out of the steppes, in Germany Hitler drew nearer to the conquest of power. Half-finished giants would be of little use in the hour of supreme danger, especially if they lacked the necessary workers. You can, by the force of enthusiasm, get a minority to work overtime even in a snow-storm to get a new factory built according to the plan. In a country like Russia such a minority may number some millions, and you will get your factories built. But you cannot by mere enthusiasm induce the average worker, freshly arrived from his village, to put forth the continuous effort essential in acquiring industrial skill, and not only to fulfil the plan, but to maintain, too, the quality of output. So one had somehow to stop the pace of "assault." What was needed was a normal economy and a normal society where work, generally speaking, was not building new factories but producing goods, and the reward for work was the power to buy a part of these goods in proportion to one's exertions.

Already in June 1931 Stalin had spoken of the necessity of working with, and duly rewarding, the old specialists who had formerly been considered as brakes on enthusiastic reconstruction, and also of increasing the average worker's interest in, and personal responsibility for, his work. After 1930 the agricultural Artel was accepted as the most suitable type of agricultural collectivization. As distinct from the agricultural Commune, which originally had been encouraged as the highest type of collectivization, the Artel leaves to its members a certain private economy, and even the right to sell the products of his private husbandry in the markets. In 1932, at last, the new tractor-building factories began to work. Now, collective agriculture could get a real technical advantage over the old methods easily understood by the average peasant. On 1 December, 1934, it became possible to abolish the rationing of bread. During 1935 the free market was restored for almost all goods, on a price-level averaging between the prices the state had asked for the guaranteed ration-minimum, and those the customer had paid to the peasants for additional goods on the kollkhos market. Now increased wages or salaries meant proportionally increased purchasing power. The Stakhanovite movement was initiated. Now the workers were encouraged not only to make temporary exertions and occasional proposals for rationalization, but to achieve a permanent increase of skill and of output, in quantity as well as in quality.

Fulfilling the Leninist Plan

BORIS N. PONOMARYOV

In 1956, at the time Khrushchev began his down-grading of Stalin, Soviet historical writing was sharply criticized for having succumbed to the "cult of personality," i.e., the glorification of Stalin. The old 1938 official history of the Communist Party of the Soviet Union, which Stalin had closely supervised, was dropped from circulation. A committee of Soviet scholars under the chairmanship of *Boris N. Ponomaryov* (1905–   ), member of the Central Committee and of the Secretariat of the Communist Party, was appointed to prepare a new text. The new work duly appeared in 1959 and was translated into English in 1960. Stalin's name has been systematically removed from any favorable connection, while credit for achievements which the authors regard as positive goes simply to "the Party." Surprisingly enough, the actual text — particularly concerning the collectivization of agriculture — has otherwise scarcely been altered from the 1938 version.

THE development of Socialist construction and vast, long-term capital investments required a higher level of economic planning. Large-scale Socialist industry, which had grown and gained strength, now played the dominant role in the economy. The Party had accumulated considerable experience in planning, and was now [in 1927] in a position to advance from annual targets to long-term plans for a number of years. This was a major victory for the Leninist economic policy of the Party.

In his last articles, devoted to the plan for building Socialism, Lenin wrote that for the first time in history the Soviet State had the opportunity "of ascertaining the period necessary for bringing about radical social changes; we now see clearly *what* can be done in five years, and what requires much more time" (*Collected Works*, Vol. 33, pp. 441–42).

From Boris N. Ponomaryov et al., *History of the Communist Party of the Soviet Union* (Moscow: Foreign Languages Publishing House, 1960), pp. 421–422, 424, 426–428, 435, 441–442, 446–449, 459–460, 474–476.

The Fifteenth Congress adopted directives for the *first Five-Year Plan* of development of the national economy.

The basic economic tasks of this plan were, as the Congress pointed out, steadily to expand large-scale Socialist industry, to use it for bringing about a rapid growth of all branches of the national economy and an increase of the share of its Socialist sector, and to squeeze out the capitalist elements more vigorously, with a view to launching a Socialist offensive against the remnants of capitalism along the whole economic front.

The adoption of directives for the first Five-Year Plan signified a new and higher stage of planning in the Soviet national economy, in the battle to build Socialism. These directives specified the schedules and rates of the great social transformations to take place in the Soviet Union. . . .

In pursuance of the Fifteenth Congress decisions, the Party with renewed force went ahead with Socialist industrialisation and preparations for the mass collectivisation of agriculture based on Lenin's plan for building Socialism in the U.S.S.R.

The Socialist reconstruction of the national economy evoked the stubborn resistance of the capitalist elements inside the country and greatly alarmed the world bourgeoisie. The imperialists and the landlords, the big industrialists and bankers who had fled the Soviet country saw in the Nepmen and the kulaks their mainstay in the bitter struggle to frustrate the building of Socialism in the U.S.S.R. . . .

The frenzied resistance of the kulaks to the measures taken by the Soviet Government in the countryside encouraged concealed enemy groups in their struggle to restore capitalism in the country. At the beginning of 1928 a big saboteur organisation consisting of bourgeois specialists was discovered in the Shakhty and in other areas of the Donets coalfield the "Shakhty case"). For several years a group of these specialists and camouflaged Whites had engaged secretly in subversive work aimed at destroying the coal industry in the

Donets coalfield, carrying out assignments of the former owners of the mines — Russian and foreign capitalists — and of foreign intelligence services. The saboteurs caused explosions in the mines and flooded them, damaged costly new equipment, set fire to power stations and deliberately misspent the people's money earmarked for capital construction. Members of this subversive organisation purchased abroad equipment for the mines and power stations that was obviously outmoded and useless. Especially dangerous were the wreckers' attempts to worsen the conditions of the miners. They deliberately disorganised the supply of food and consumer goods to the miners and their families, cheated the workers in paying wages, held up housing programmes and infringed safety rules in the mines, which endangered the lives of the miners. The underlying purpose was to cause discontent among the workers and turn them against the Party and the Soviet Government.

The wreckers also aimed at undermining the defence of the country and clearing the way to intervention by the imperialist Powers. Nearly 300 one-time big capitalists and nobles were among the saboteurs exposed in the "Shakhty case." . . .

The difficulties encountered in Socialist reconstruction, and the inevitable sharpening of the class struggle as a result of the Socialist offensive, gave rise to vacillations among the petty-bourgeois strata of the population. There were echoes of this also in the Party. A group of Right-wing defeatists took shape. As early as 1925 Bukharin had proclaimed the slogan "Enrich yourselves!" In practice this slogan signified a policy of support for the kulak farms in the countryside. But when the Party was engaged in combating the Trotskyists and Zinovievites as the main danger, the Right-wingers, carefully concealing their differences with the Party, had been lying low, making a show of fighting against the Trotskyists. But when the Party launched its decisive offensive against the kulaks, the leaders of the Right wingers—Bukharin, Rykov and Tomsky—openly came out against the policy of Socialist industrialisation and the collectivisation of agriculture.

While admitting in words that it was possible to build Socialism in the U.S.S.R., the Right opportunists in fact resisted the policy of the all-out expansion of heavy industry. They opposed rapid rates of industrialisation.

The Right-wingers opposed the all-out Socialist offensive along the whole front and the liquidation of the capitalist elements in the national economy. They opposed the offensive against the kulaks. At a time when the capitalist elements were waging a fierce struggle against the construction of Socialism, the Right-wingers propounded the "theory" that the class struggle in the country was subsiding and that the kulaks could peacefully grow into Socialism. They refused to admit that the broad highway to Socialism in the countryside was, as Lenin taught, the producer co-operation in its highest form—the collective farm. Lenin's co-operative plan could not be put into effect unless the kulaks were eliminated as a class. The Right-wingers held that the countryside could be directed along Socialist lines only through the marketing and purchasing co-operatives. They suggested giving "free rein" to spontaneous development of the market and removing all restrictions on kulak farming. Abandoning Lenin's concept of the class struggle and the dictatorship of the proletariat, the Right-wingers would have the Party and State organisations make direct concessions to the capitalist elements.

Thus, in practice, they denied that Socialism could be built in the U.S.S.R. In the Party they spread the *ideology of defeatism* in the face of difficulties, and sought an *agreement* with the kulak and capitalist elements in town and country. Their stand ultimately meant the restoration of capitalism. The Central Committee rallied the Party and the working class for a decisive struggle against the Right-wing defeatists, now the main danger in the Party, the mouthpiece of the anti-Soviet forces in the country and a weapon of the capitalist encirclement. . . .

Industrialisation was carried out with a truly Bolshevik élan, such as the world had never seen before. The working class provided splendid examples of labour valour. The scale and the rate of construction in the U.S.S.R. astonished the world. Enemies asserted that the targets planned by the Party would never be reached and foretold the failure of the Soviet plans. The working people in all countries were gladdened by the successes of the Soviet Union.

The vast scale of industrialisation and the heroism displayed by the working class exerted a strong influence on the masses of the working peasantry. They saw that the Party and the Government, overcoming difficulties, were building factories to make tractors and new farm machines. Numerous peasant delegations visited the new factories and construction sites, attended workers' meetings and were inspired by their enthusiasm. Upon returning to their villages the advanced representatives of the working peasantry took the initiative in setting up new collective farms. The organised workers of industrial enterprises and building sites assumed patronage over rural areas, and sent numerous workers' teams to the countryside.

That was how the mass movement for joining the collective farms was prepared and began, a movement which grew into solid collectivisation. The peasantry turned to the Socialist path of development, to the collective-farm path. The middle peasants followed the poor peasants into the collective farms. . . .

While the whole capitalist world was in the grip of the economic crisis, the U.S.S.R. was steadily proceeding with Socialist construction. The average annual increase of its industrial output in the first two years of the Five-Year Plan was about 20 per cent.

Along with the rapid growth of industry, the mass collective-farm movement was under way in the country. By the beginning of 1930 the five-year programme of collective-farm development had, in the main, been fulfilled. A number of regions became regions of *solid collectivisation*, when the peasants of whole villages, districts and areas joined the collective farms. In 124 districts more than 70 per cent of all the peasant farms were collectivised. The largest number of districts of solid collectivisation were in the Volga region, the North Caucasus and the steppe part of Ukraine.

The transition to solid collectivisation signified a *radical turn* of the bulk of the peasantry towards Socialism. Prior to the mass collective-farm movement there were 24.5 million individual peasant farms in the U.S.S.R., of which about 8.5 million belonged to poor peasants, 15 million to middle peasants and more than one million to kulaks. The poor and middle peasants together constituted the most numerous labouring class in the U.S.S.R. Though petty peasant commodity economy was not of a capitalist nature, it was essentially of the same type, since it based itself on private property in the means of production and engendered kulak capitalists from its midst. When joining the collective farms, the peasants socialised the basic means of production. The working peasantry was abandoning the old path of development which spontaneously engendered capitalism and led to the enslavement of the poor and middle peasants by the kulaks; it was taking a new, Socialist path, free of kulak bondage and capitalist exploitation. A Socialist, collective-farm system was being established in the countryside. . . .

The development of the Socialist sector of the national economy, the new alignment of class forces in the country and the possession by the State of its own grain-producing base—the collective and State farms—enabled the Party to proceed at the end of 1929 from the policy of restricting and squeezing out the kulaks to the policy of eliminating them as a class on the basis of solid collectivisation. The essence of this policy was to *deprive the kulak class of the means of production essential for its existence and development*, namely, the free use of land, the instruments of production, the renting of land and the right to hire labour. This policy was legislatively embodied in a number of decisions adopted by the higher organs of the Soviet State. In districts of solid collectivisation the laws on the renting of land and the hiring of labour on individual peasant farms were repealed.

Solid collectivisation meant that all the land in the area of a particular village passed into the hands of a collective farm. All kulak plots in this land were transferred to the collective farm. Thus the kulaks were deprived not only of the right to rent any land, but also of those plots of land which had been used by them previously. The nationalisation of the land accomplished as a result of the October Revolution made possible such surveying and demarcation of the lands as benefited the collective farms. Lenin pointed out that the nationalisation of the land gave "the proletarian State the maximum opportunity of passing to Socialism in agriculture" (*Collected Works*, Vol. 28, p. 291). The collective farms did not have to make any redemption payments to the peasants for their plots of land, or to recompense them for the lands which were passing into collective use. Thus the absence of private property in land in the U.S.S.R. facilitated the Socialist reconstruction of the countryside and the struggle against the kulaks.

The collectivisation of agriculture proceeded in bitter class struggle with the kulaks, in conditions of a hostile capitalist encirclement. The kulaks carried on malicious propaganda against the collective-farm movement, spread all kinds of provocative rumours, set fire to collective-farm buildings, poisoned the livestock, damaged tractors and other machines, assassinated rural Communists, chairmen of collective farms, rural newspaper correspondents and village activists. They did everything in their power to prevent the peasants from joining the collective farms and to frustrate collectivisation. The entry of the majority of the peasantry into the collective farms on a mass scale was therefore accompanied by a decisive struggle against the kulaks. The peasants demanded the complete expropriation of the kulaks and their expulsion from the villages.

Supporting in every way the struggle of the poor and middle peasants against the kulaks, the Soviet Government lifted the ban on expropriation of the kulaks. Local organs of Soviet power in the districts of solid collectivisation were granted the right to evict the most malicious kulaks to districts far removed from their places of residence and to confiscate all their means of production (cattle, machines and other farm property), transferring them to the possession of collective farms. The kulaks were completely expropriated. This was the only way to deal with the kulaks. These measures fully met the interests of Socialist construction, and ensured the success of the collective-farm movement and the consolidation of the collective farms.

Thus, at the very beginning of the mass building of collective farms the Central Committee of the Party, proceeding from Lenin's teachings on co-operation, gave the Party, the working class and the working peasantry a concrete plan of struggle for the victory of the collective-farm system. . . .

January and February, 1930, were months of headlong growth of the collective farms. The movement for solid collectivisation embraced ever new regions of the country. During this period about 10 million peasant households joined the collective farms.

But along with real progress in collectivisation, there were also unhealthy signs. There turned out to be certain distortions of Party policy in collectivisation, distortions which caused discontent among the middle peasants.

Above all, the Leninist voluntary principle of forming collective farms was being violated. Not infrequently patient organising and explanatory work was being replaced by mere injunctions and coercion against the middle peasants. Voluntary entry into collective farms was being replaced by compulsion, on pain of being "dekulakised," disfranchised, and so on. In some districts as many as 15 per cent of the peasants were "dekulakised" and from 15 to 20 per cent disfranchised.

The Party's directive concerning the agricultural artel as the chief form of the collective-farm movement was also being violated. In a number of places attempts were made to skip the artel form and pass straight to the commune by collectivising small livestock, poultry, etc. . . .

The enemies of Soviet power, and above all the kulaks, tried to take advantage of these mistakes and excesses committed by Party organisations. Former Whites, Socialist-Revolutionaries and other hidden anti-Soviet elements raised their heads again. The enemy acted with craft and cunning. Every device was used—from provocation to brutal assassination of Communists and active non-Party people in the villages. The class enemies instigated the peasants to slaughter their animals before entering the collective farms, spreading the rumour that all the livestock would be taken away anyhow. Giving way to this provocation of the kulaks, many peasants slaughtered their cows, pigs, sheep and poultry. In the economic year 1929/30 the number of head of cattle in the country decreased by 14.6 million, pigs by one-third, sheep and goats by more than a quarter. Almost all this livestock was slaughtered mainly in February and March, 1930. As a result of these hostile actions of the kulaks and their toadies, animal husbandry in the U.S.S.R. suffered a heavy loss from which it could not recover for a long time. . . .

In conditions of the colossal construction during the years of the first Five-Year Plan the country had to put up with many privations and hardships. It was still a poor country. There was a shortage of clothing, footwear, and many other articles of primary necessity. At the construction sites the workers lived in tents and temporary wooden barracks. Foodstuffs and many manufactured goods were strictly rationed. All these difficulties were shouldered primarily by the working class. But the workers realised that, in conditions of a hostile capitalist encirclement, there was no other way of transforming their country into a mighty industrial Power. They understood that industry could be built up only at the cost of sacrifice and the most rigorous economy. Stinting themselves in everything, and tightening their belts, the workers displayed unprecedented labour heroism. The working class and all the working people were firmly convinced of the victory of Socialism in the U.S.S.R., of the correctness of the policy of the Party; and they advanced unswervingly towards their goal. The unity, high degree of organisation and selflessness of the working class exerted a tremendous moral influence on the poor and middle peasants who were developing the collective-farm movement. Particularly great was the labour enthusiasm of the youth. In response to the appeal of the Party, tens of thousands of young people were sent by the Young Communist League organisations to work in still undeveloped localities, and to construction sites in the Urals, Kuznetsk coalfield, Donets coalfield, Far East and Central Asia.

Mobilising the creative activity of the working class for the fulfillment of the Five-Year Plan in four years, the Central Committee of the Party in September, 1930, addressed an appeal to the workers calling on them to organise Socialist emulation for successful fulfillment of the targets of the third year of the Five-Year Plan. There was not a single enterprise where the workers did not respond to this appeal of the Party. The Socialist emulation movement developed with still greater force throughout the country. The at-

mosphere of the factories changed, and with it their habitual tenor of life. Workers at kindred construction sites, factories and plants began to exchange their labour experience, while production reviews and competitions for the best shop and workers' team were organised in the individual factories. New indices of the work of advanced workers' teams and shock workers appeared on the boards of honour in factories and at construction sites. The number of heroes of labour steadily grew. . . .

At the beginning of 1933 the glad news spread throughout the country that the first Five-Year Plan had been fulfilled ahead of time—in four years and three months. In January, 1933, a joint plenary meeting of the Central Committee and Central Control Commission of the Party reviewed the results of the Five-Year Plan. It noted the following major results:

The U.S.S.R. had been converted from an agrarian into an *industrial* country. The Socialist system had completely eliminated the capitalist elements in industry and had become the sole economic system. In 1932 the volume of output of large-scale industry exceeded the pre-war level more than threefold, and that of 1928 more than twofold. Its proportion of the total output of the national economy had risen to 70 per cent. The U.S.S.R. had created its own advanced technical basis which had made possible the reconstruction of all branches of the national economy. During the first Five-Year Plan period 1,500 new industrial enterprises had been put into operation. A number of new industries had been built up, such as an up-to-date iron and steel industry, a tractor industry, an automobile industry, a chemical industry, and an aircraft industry. A new coal and metallurgical base had been created in the east, the Urals-Kuzbas base. The output of electric power had increased by more than 150 per cent. The economic independence of the country had been strengthened: the U.S.S.R. had now begun to produce most necessary industrial equipment at its own enterprises. The

Soviet Union had strengthened its defence capacity.

In agriculture, as a result of the determined swing of the poor and middle peasants towards Socialism, the collective and State farms had become the predominant force. A *collective-farm system,* large-scale Socialist farming, had been created in the countryside. From a country of petty peasant farming the U.S.S.R. had become a country where agriculture was run on the largest scale in the world. A leap from an old qualitative state to a new qualitative state had taken place in agriculture. The elimination of the kulaks as a class had been carried out on the basis of solid collectivisation. The machine-and-tractor stations, equipped with tractors and the most up-to-date agricultural machinery, had become important levers in reorganising agriculture along Socialist lines. The agricultural artel had become the principal form of the collective-farm movement.

The progress of Socialism in all spheres of the national economy had brought about a *radical improvement in the material conditions of the working people.* Unemployment in the towns, this scourge of the working class of all capitalist countries, had been completely abolished in the U.S.S.R. The collective-farm system had put an end to kulak bondage and to impoverishment of the working peasantry. The poor peasants and the lower stratum of the middle peasants had been raised to a level of material security in the collective farms. The growth of the national income and the improvement of the material conditions of the working people had been accompanied by a marked rise of their cultural level and the rapid growth of a new, Soviet intelligentsia.

The foundations of Socialism had been laid in the Soviet Union. As in the towns, the Socialist form of economy had firmly established itself in the countryside, too. The question: "Who will beat whom?", posed by Lenin, had been settled in favour of Socialism. Radical changes had taken place in the class structure of Soviet society. The capitalist elements in the country had, in the main, been eliminated. The social basis of the dictatorship of the proletariat had been extended and consolidated. The collective-farm peasantry had become the firm *mainstay* of Soviet power. This was already a *new* class, building a new life on the basis of collective ownership of the means of production. The alliance of the working class and peasantry had undergone a change in aspect, and had acquired a new content. Lenin's wise policy of an alliance between the working class and the poor peasants, on the one hand, and the middle peasants, on the other, had helped to draw the bulk of the peasantry into Socialist construction and had ensured victory over the capitalist elements. The alliance of the working class and collective-farm peasantry was being established on a *new basis—the community* of their interests in the building, consolidation and development of Socialism in town and country.

This was an *epoch-making* victory of the working class, working peasantry and intelligentsia of the U.S.S.R., won under the leadership of the Communist Party.

The results of the first Five-Year Plan were of tremendous international significance.

The Soviet Union had demonstrated to the whole world the superiority of the planned Socialist system of economy over the capitalist system, strengthened its economic might and independence and become an important factor in international affairs.

The fulfilment of the Five-Year Plan exerted a revolutionising influence on the working masses of the capitalist countries. The alignment of class forces markedly changed in favour of Socialism. The results of the Five-Year Plan raised the revolutionary spirit of the working class all over the world and strengthened its confidence in ultimate victory.

Even the enemies of the Soviet Union had to admit the success of the Five-Year Plan. The predictions of the world bourgeoisie and its agents about its inevitable failure had proved false. The working class and the working peasantry of the U.S.S.R. had proved that they could manage without landlords, capitalists and kulaks, that they could create a new and better Socialist system, which knew no crises and unemployment and ensured a continuous improvement in their material and cultural well-being.

The Logic of Totalitarianism

RUDOLF HILFERDING

Rudolf Hilferding (1877–1941) was an eminent theorist of democratic Marxism and a leader of the German Social Democratic Party. He served as Finance Minister of the German Republic in 1928 and 1929. He fled Germany when Hitler came to power, but in 1941 the Nazis arrested him in France and executed him.

In 1940 Hilferding wrote a brief but incisive article on the nature of the Soviet system, by way of replying to the suggestion of the British socialist, R. L. Worrall, that Soviet Russia had become a form of "state capitalism." Hilferding's analysis was first published in Russian in the *Sotsialistichesky Vestnik* (Socialist Messenger, New York); later on English version appeared in the *Modern Review* of New York. Hilferding concluded that totalitarianism — Communist or Fascist — was a fundamentally new kind of economic system, neither capitalist nor socialist.

T HE concept of "state capitalism" can scarcely pass the test of serious economic analysis. Once the state becomes the exclusive owner of all means of production, the functioning of a capitalist economy is rendered impossible by destruction of the mechanism which keeps the life-blood of such a system circulating. A capitalist economy is a market economy. Prices, which result from competition among capitalist owners (it is this competition that "in the last instance" gives rise to the law of value), determine what and how much is produced, what fraction of the profit is accumulated, and in what particular branches of production this accumulation occurs. They also determine how in an economy, which has to overcome crises again and again, proportionate relations among the various branches of production are reestablished whether in the case of simple or expanded reproduction.

A capitalist economy is governed by the laws of the market (analyzed by Marx) and the autonomy of these laws constitutes the decisive symptom of the capitalist system of production. A state economy, however, eliminates precisely the autonomy of economic laws. It represents not a market but a consumers' economy. It is no longer price but rather a state planning commission that now determines what is produced and how. Formally, prices and wages still exist, but their function is no longer the same; they no longer determine the process of production which is now controlled by a central power that fixes

From Rudolf Hilferding, "State Capitalism or Totalitarian State Economy," translated by Nina Stein, *Modern Review* (June 1947), pp. 266–271 (entire text). Reprinted by permission of the American Labor Conference on International Affairs, publisher of the *Modern Review*.

prices and wages. Prices and wages become means of distribution which determine the share that the individual receives out of the sum total of products that the central power places at the disposal of society. They now constitute a technical form of distribution which is simpler than direct individual allotment of products which no longer can be classed as merchandise. Prices have become symbols of distribution and no longer comprise a regulating factor in the economy. While maintaining the form, a complete transformation of function has occurred.

Both the "stimulating fire of competition" and the passionate striving for profit, which provide the basic incentive of capitalist production, die out. Profit means individual appropriation of surplus products and is therefore possible only on the basis of private ownership. But, objects Mr. Worrall, did Marx not consider accumulation as an essential ear-mark of capitalism and does not accumulation play a decisive role in the Russian economy? Is that not state capitalism?

Mr. Worrall has overlooked one slight detail; namely, that Marx refers to the accumulation of *capital,* of an ever-increasing amount of the means of production which produce profit and the appropriation of which supplies the driving force to capitalist production. In other words, he refers to the accumulation of value which creates surplus value; i.e., a specifically *capitalist* process of expanding economic activity.

On the other hand, the accumulation of means of production and of products is so far from being a specific feature of capitalism that it plays a decisive part in all economic systems, except perhaps in the most primitive collecting of food. In a consumer economy, in an economy organized by the state, there is not accumulation of values but of consumers' goods — products that the central power wants in order to satisfy consumers' need. The mere fact that the Russian state economy accumulates does not make it a capitalist economy, for it is

not capital that is being accumulated. Mr. Worrall's argument is based on a gross confusion between value and use value. And he really believes that a socialist economy could do without accumulation!

But what then (and here we come to the basic question) is that central power that rules over the Russian economy? Trotsky and Worrall reply: "Bureaucracy." But while Trotsky refuses to consider the bureaucracy as a class (according to Marx a class is characterized by the place it occupies in the process of production), Worrall makes an amazing discovery. Soviet bureaucracy in its structure (which unfortunately he does not analyze) differs "basically" from any other bourgeoisie, but its function remains the same — the accumulation of capital. The fact that, despite great structural differences, the function can remain unchanged is, of course, a miracle that cannot occur in nature but seems (according to Worrall) possible in human society.

In any case, Worrall accepts this as evidence that Russia is dominated by a bourgeois class and thus by state capitalism. He clings obstinately to his confusion of capital and the means of production and seems unable to conceive of any form of accumulation other than capitalist accumulation. He fails to understand that accumulation (i.e. the expansion of production) in any economic system is the task of the managers of production; that even in an ideal socialist system this accumulation can result only from the surplus product (which only under capitalism takes the form of surplus value), and that the fact of accumulation in itself does not prove the capitalist nature of an economy.

But does the "bureaucracy" really "rule" the economy and consequently the people? Bureaucracy everywhere, and particularly in the Soviet Union, is composed of a conglomeration of the most varied elements. To it belong not only government officials in the narrow sense of the word (i.e. from minor employees up to the generals and even Stalin himself) but also the directors of all branches of industry and such functionaries as, for example, the postal and railway employees. How could this variegated lot possibly achieve a unified rule? Who are its representatives? How does it adopt decisions? What organs are at its disposal?

In reality, the "bureaucracy" is not an independent bearer of power. In accordance with its structure as well as function, it is only an instrument in the hands of the real rulers. It is organized as an hierarchy and subordinated to the commanding power. It receives but does not give orders. Any functionary, as Trotsky justly puts it, "can be sacrificed by his superior in the hierarchical system in order to decrease any kind of dissatisfaction." And these are the new masters of production, the substitute for capitalists! Stalin thoroughly exploded this myth when, during the last purges, he ordered shot, among others, thousands of industrial managers.

It is not the bureaucracy that rules, but he who gives orders to the bureaucracy. And it is Stalin who gives orders to the Russian bureaucracy. Lenin and Trotsky with a select group of followers who were never able to come to independent decisions as a party but always remained an instrument in the hands of the leaders (the same was true later with the fascist and national-socialist parties) seized power at a time when the old state apparatus was collapsing. They changed the state apparatus to suit their needs as rulers, eliminating democracy and establishing their own dictatorship which in their ideology, but by no means in practice, was identified with the "dictatorship of the proletariat." Thus they created the first *totalitarian state* — even before the name was invented. Stalin carried on with the job, removing his rivals through the instrument of the state apparatus and establishing an unlimited personal dictatorship.

This is the reality which should not be obscured by construing alleged domination by a "bureaucracy" which is in fact subordinate to the government to the same extent as are the rest of the people. This is true even though some modest crumbs from the master's table may be doled out to it — without, of course, a guarantee that other crumbs are to follow and at the price of constant danger to their very lives. Their material share does not constitute any important portion of the social product. Nevertheless, the psychological effect of such a differentiation may be quite considerable.

Important economic consequences flow from this fact. It is the essence of a totalitarian state that it subjects the economy to its aims. The economy is deprived of its own laws, it becomes a controlled economy. Once this control is effected, it transforms the market economy into a consumers' economy. The character and extent of needs are then determined by the state. The German and Italian economies provide evidence of the fact that such control, once initiated in a totalitarian state, spreads rapidly and tends to become all-embracing as was the case in Russia from the very beginning. Despite great differences in their points of departure, the economic system of totalitarian states are drawing close to each other. In Germany, too, the state, striving to maintain and strengthen its power, determines the character of production and accumulation. Prices lose their regulating function and become merely means of distribution. The economy, and with it the exponents of economic activity, are more or less subjected to the state, becoming its subordinates. The economy loses the primacy which it held under bourgeois society. This does not mean, however, that economic circles do not have great influence on the ruling power in Germany as well as in Russia. But their influence is conditional, has limits and is not decisive in relation to the essence of policy. Policy is actually determined by a small circle of those who are in power. It is their interests, their ideas as to what is required to maintain, exploit, and strengthen their own power that determines the policy which they impose as law upon the subordinated economy. This is why the subjective factor, the "unforeseeable," "irrational" character of political development has gained such importance in politics.

The faithful believe only in heaven and hell as determining forces; the Marxist sectarian only in capitalism and socialism, in classes — bourgeoisie and proletariat. The Marxist sectarian cannot grasp the idea that present-day state power, having achieved independence, is unfolding its enormous strength according to its own laws, subjecting social forces and compelling them to serve its ends for a short or long period of time.

Therefore neither the Russian nor the totalitarian system in general is determined by the character of the economy. On the contrary, it is the economy that is determined by the policy of the ruling power and subjected to the aims and purposes of this power. The totalitarian power lives by the economy, but not for the economy or even for the class ruling the economy — as is the case of the bourgeois state, though the latter (as any student of foreign policy can demonstrate) may occasionally pursue aims of its own. An analogy to the totalitarian state may be found in the era of the late Roman Empire, in the regime of the Praetorians and their emperors.

Of course, from a social democratic viewpoint the Bolshevik economy can hardly be called "socialist," for to us socialism is indissolubly linked to democracy. According to our concept, socialization of the means of production implies freeing the economy from the rule of one class and vesting it in society as a whole — a society which is democratically self-governed. We never imagined that the political form of that "managed economy" which was to replace capitalist production for a free market could be unrestricted absolutism. The correlation between the economic basis and the political structure seemed to us a very definite one: namely, that the socialist society would inaugurate the highest realization of democracy. Even those among us who believed that the strictest application of centralized power would be necessary or inevitable for the period of transition, considered this period only temporary and bound to end after the suppression of the propertied classes. Together with the disappearance of classes, class rule was also to vanish — that class rule which we considered the only possible form of political rule in general. "The state is withering away . . ."

But history, this "best of all Marxists," has taught us differently. It has taught us that "administering of things," despite Engels' expectations, may turn into unlimited "administering of people," and thus not only lead to the emancipation of the state from the economy but even to the subjection of the economy to the state.

Once subjected to the state, the economy secures the continued existence of this form of government. The fact that such a result flows from a unique situation primarily brought about by war does not exclude a Marxist analysis, but it alters somewhat our rather simplified and schematic conception of the correlation between economy and state and between economy and politics which developed in a completely different period. The emergence of the state as an independent power greatly complicates the economic characterization of a society in which politics (i.e. the state) plays a determining and decisive role.

For this reason the controversy as to whether the economic system of the Soviet Union is "capitalist" or "socialist" seems to me rather pointless. It is neither. It represents a *totalitarian state economy*, i.e. a system to which the economics of Germany and Italy are drawing closer and closer.

Soviet Bonapartism

LEON TROTSKY

Leon Trotsky (1879–1940), one-time second-in-command to Lenin, defeated by Stalin in the controversies of the 1920's, is the great tragic figure of the Russian Revolution. He was expelled from the Communist Party in 1927 and deported from Russia in 1929. He finally settled in Mexico, where, in 1940, he was assassinated by a Soviet agent. During the years of exile Trotsky published a steady stream of articles and books, attacking Stalin's rule in Russia as a bureaucratic and "Bonapartist" perversion of the Russian Revolution analogous to the rule of Napoleon Bonaparte in France.

OWING to the insignificance of the Russian bourgeoisie, the democratic tasks of backward Russia — such as liquidation of the monarchy and the semi-feudal slavery of the peasants — could be achieved only through a dictatorship of the proletariat. The proletariat, however, having seized the power at the head of the peasant masses, could not stop at the achievement of these democratic tasks. The bourgeois revolution was directly bound up with the first stages of a socialist revolution. That fact was not accidental. The history of recent decades very clearly shows that, in the conditions of capitalist decline, backward countries are unable to attain that level which the old centers of capitalism have attained. Having themselves arrived in a blind alley, the highly civilized nations block the road to those in process of civilization. Russia took the road of proletarian revolution, not because her economy was the first to become ripe for a socialist change, but because she could not develop further on a capitalist basis. Socialization of the means of production had become a necessary condition for bringing the country out of barbarism.

That is the *law of combined development* for backward countries. Entering upon the socialist revolution as "the weakest link in the capitalist chain" (Lenin), the former empire of the tzars is even now, in the nineteenth year after the revolution, still confronted with the task of "catching up with and outstripping" — consequently in the first place *catching up with* — Europe and America. She has, that is, to solve those problems of technique and productivity which were long ago solved by capitalism in the advanced countries.

Could it indeed be otherwise? The overthrow of the old ruling classes did not achieve, but only completely revealed, the task: to rise from barbarism to culture. At the same time, by concentrating the means of production in the hands of the state, the revolution made it possible to apply new and incomparably more effective industrial methods. Only thanks to a planned directive was it possible in so brief a span to restore what had been destroyed by the imperialist and civil wars, to create gigantic new enterprises, to introduce new kinds of production and establish new branches of industry.

From Leon Trotsky, *The Revolution Betrayed: What Is the Soviet Union and Where Is It Going?*, translated by Max Eastman (Garden City, N.Y.: Doubleday, Doran and Co., 1937), pp. 5–8, 19–20, 45–47, 54–56, 275–279. Reprinted by permission of Pioneer Publishers of New York.

The extraordinary tardiness in the development of the international revolution, upon whose prompt aid the leaders of the Bolshevik party had counted, created immense difficulties for the Soviet Union, but also revealed its inner powers and resources. However, a correct appraisal of the results achieved — their grandeur as well as their inadequacy — is possible only with the help of an international scale of measurement. . . .

. . . During the last three years the production of iron has doubled. The production of steel and of the rolling mills has increased almost 2½ times. The output of oil, coal and iron has increased from 3 to 3½ times the pre-war figure. In 1920, when the first plan of electrification was drawn up, there were ten district power stations in the country with a total power production of 253,000 kilowatts. In 1935, there were already ninety-five of these stations with a total power of 4,345,000 kilowatts. In 1925, the Soviet Union stood eleventh in the production of electroenergy; in 1935, it was second only to Germany and the United States. In the production of coal, the Soviet Union has moved forward from tenth to fourth place. In steel, from sixth to third place. In the production of tractors, to the first place in the world. This also is true of the production of sugar.

Gigantic achievements in industry, enormously promising beginnings in agriculture, an extraordinary growth of the old industrial cities and a building of new ones, a rapid increase of the number of workers, a rise in cultural level and cultural demands — such are the indubitable results of the October revolution, in which the prophets of the old world tried to see the grave of human civilization. With the bourgeois economists we have no longer anything to quarrel over. Socialism has demonstrated its right to victory, not on the pages of *Das Kapital,* but in an industrial arena comprising a sixth part of the earth's surface — not in the language of dialectics, but in the language of steel, cement and electricity. Even if the Soviet Union, as a result of internal difficulties, external blows and the mistakes of its leadership, were to collapse — which we firmly hope will not happen — there would remain as an earnest of the future this indestructible fact, that thanks solely to a proletarian revolution a backward country has achieved in less than ten years successes unexampled in history. . . .

. . . The national income per person in the Soviet Union is considerably less than in the West. And since capital investment consumes about 25 to 30 per cent, — incomparably more than anywhere else — the total amount consumed by the popular mass cannot but be considerably lower than in the advanced capitalist countries.

To be sure, in the Soviet Union there are no possessing classes, whose extravagance is balanced by an underconsumption of the popular mass. However the weight of this corrective is not so great as might appear at first glance. The fundamental evil of the capitalist system is not the extravagance of the possessing classes, however disgusting that may be in itself, but the fact that in order to guarantee its right to extravagance the bourgeoisie maintains its private ownership of the means of production, thus condemning the economic system to anarchy and decay. In the matter of luxuries the bourgeoisie, of course, has a monopoly of consumption. But in things of prime necessity, the toiling masses constitute the overwhelming majority of consumers. We shall see later, moreover, that although the Soviet Union has no possessing classes in the proper sense of the word, still she has very privileged commanding strata of the population, who appropriate the lion's share in the sphere of consumption. And so if there is a lower per capita production of things of prime necessity in the Soviet Union than in the advanced capitalist countries, that does mean that the standard of living of the Soviet masses still falls below the capitalist level.

The historic responsibility for this situation lies, of course, upon Russia's black and heavy past, her heritage of darkness and poverty. There was no other way out upon the road of progress except through the overthrow of capitalism. To convince yourself of this, it is only necessary to cast a glance at the Baltic countries and Poland, once the most advanced parts of the tzar's empire, and now hardly emerging from the morass. The undying service of the Soviet regime lies in its intense and successful struggle with Russia's thousand-year-old backwardness. But a correct estimate of what has been attained is the first condition for further progress.

The Soviet regime is passing through a *preparatory* stage, importing, borrowing and appropriating the technical and cultural conquests of the West. The comparative coefficients of production and consumption testify that this preparatory stage is far from finished. Even under the improbable condition of a continuing complete capitalist standstill, it must still occupy a whole historic period. . . .

The material premise of communism should be so high a development of the economic powers of man that productive labor, having ceased to be a burden, will not require any goad, and the distribution of life's goods, existing in continual abundance, will not demand — as it does not now in any well-off family or "decent" boardinghouse — any control except that of education, habit and social opinion. Speaking frankly, I think it would be pretty dull-witted to consider such a really modest perspective "utopian."

Capitalism prepared the conditions and forces for a social revolution: technique, science and the proletariat. The communist structure cannot, however, immediately replace the bourgeois society. The material and cultural inheritance from the past is wholly inadequate for that. In its first steps the workers' state cannot yet permit everyone to work "according to his abilities" — that is, as much as he can and wishes to — nor can it reward everyone "according to his needs," regardless of the work he does. In order to increase the productive forces, it is necessary to resort to the customary norms of wage payment — that is, to the distribution of life's goods in proportion to the quantity and quality of individual labor.

Marx named this first stage of the new society "the lowest stage of communism," in distinction from the highest, where together with the last phantoms of want material inequality will disappear. In this sense socialism and communism are frequently contrasted as the lower and higher stages of the new society. "We have not yet, of course, *complete* communism," reads the present official Soviet doctrine, "but we have already achieved socialism — that is, the *lowest* stage of communism." In proof of this, they adduce the dominance of the state trusts in industry, the collective farms in agriculture, the state and cooperative enterprises in commerce. At first glance this gives a complete correspondence with the *a priori* — and therefore hypothetical — scheme of Marx. But it is exactly for the Marxist that this question is not exhausted by a consideration of forms of property regardless of the achieved productivity of labor. By the lowest stage of communism Marx meant, at any rate, a society which from the very beginning stands higher in its economic development than the most advanced capitalism. Theoretically such a conception is flawless, for taken *on a world scale* communism, even in its first incipient stage, means a higher level of development than that of bourgeois society. Moreover, Marx expected that the Frenchman would begin the social revolution, the German continue it, the Englishman finish it; and as to the Russian, Marx left him far in the rear. But this conceptual order was upset by the facts. Whoever tries now mechanically to apply the universal historic conception of Marx to the particular case of the Soviet

Union at the given stage of its development, will be entangled at once in hopeless contradictions.

Russia was not the strongest, but the weakest link in the chain of capitalism. The present Soviet Union does not stand above the world level of economy, but is only trying to catch up to the capitalist countries. If Marx called that society which was to be formed upon the basis of a socialization of the productive forces of the most advanced capitalism of its epoch, the lowest stage of communism, then this designation obviously does not apply to the Soviet Union, which is still today considerably poorer in technique, culture and the good things of life than the capitalist countries. It would be truer, therefore, to name the present Soviet regime in all its contradictoriness, not a socialist regime, but a *preparatory* regime *transitional* from capitalism to socialism. . . .

. . . Experience revealed what theory was unable clearly to foresee. If for the defense of socialized property against bourgeois counterrevolution a "state of armed workers" was fully adequate, it was a very different matter to regulate inequalities in the sphere of consumption. Those deprived of property are not inclined to create and defend it. The majority cannot concern itself with the privileges of the minority. For the defense of "bourgeois law" the workers' state was compelled to create a "bourgeois" type of instrument — that is, the same old gendarme, although in a new uniform.

We have thus taken the first step toward understanding the fundamental contradiction between Bolshevik program and Soviet reality. If the state does not die away, but grows more and more despotic, if the plenipotentiaries of the working class become bureaucratized, and the bureaucracy rises above the new society, this is not for some secondary reasons like the psychological relics of the past, etc., but is a result of the iron necessity to give birth to and support a privileged minority so long as it is impossible to guarantee genuine equality.

The tendencies of bureaucratism, which strangles the workers' movement in capitalist countries, would everywhere show themselves even after a proletarian revolution. But it is perfectly obvious that the poorer the society which issues from a revolution, the sterner and more naked would be the expression of this "law," the more crude would be the forms assumed by bureaucratism, and the more dangerous would it become for socialist development. The Soviet state is prevented not only from dying away, but even from freeing itself of the bureaucratic parasite, not by the "relics" of former ruling classes, as declares the naked police doctrine of Stalin, for these relics are powerless in themselves. It is prevented by immeasurably mightier factors, such as material want, cultural backwardness and the resulting dominance of "bourgeois law" in what most immediately and sharply touches every human being, the business of insuring his personal existence. . . .

While the growth of industry and the bringing of agriculture into the sphere of state planning vastly complicates the tasks of leadership, bringing to the front the problem of *quality*, bureaucratism destroys the creative initiative and the feeling of responsibility without which there is not, and cannot be, qualitative progress. The ulcers of bureaucratism are perhaps not so obvious in the big industries, but they are devouring, together with the co-operatives, the light and food-producing industries, the collective farms, the small local industries — that is, all those branches of economy which stand nearest to the people.

The progressive role of the Soviet bureaucracy coincides with the period devoted to introducing into the Soviet Union the most important elements of capitalist technique. The rough work of borrowing, imitating, transplanting and grafting, was accomplished on the bases laid down by the revolution. There was, thus far, no question of any new word in the sphere of technique, science or art. It is possible to build gigantic factories according to a ready-made Western pattern by bureaucratic command — although, to be sure, at triple the normal cost. But the farther you go, the more the economy runs into the problem of quality, which slips out of the hands of a bureaucracy like a shadow. The Soviet products are as though branded with the gray label of indifference. Under a nationalized economy, *quality* demands a democracy of producers and consumers, freedom of criticism and initiative — conditions incompatible with a totalitarian regime of fear, lies and flattery.

Behind the question of quality stands a more complicated and grandiose problem which may be comprised in the concept of *independent, technical* and *cultural creation*. The ancient philosopher said that strife is the father of all things. No new values can be created where a free conflict of ideas is impossible. To be sure, a revolutionary dictatorship means by its very essence strict limitations of freedom. But for that very reason epochs of revolution have never been directly favorable to cultural creation: they have only cleared the arena for it. The dictatorship of the proletariat opens a wider scope to human genius the more it ceases to be a dictatorship. The socialist culture will flourish only in proportion to the dying away of the state. In that simple and unshakable historic law is contained the death sentence of the present political regime in the Soviet Union. Soviet democracy is not the demand of an abstract policy, still less an abstract moral. It has become a life-and-death need of the country.

If the new state had no other interests than the interests of society, the dying away of the function of compulsion would gradually acquire a painless character. But the state is not pure spirit. Specific functions have created specific organs. The bureaucracy taken as a whole is concerned not so much with its function as with the tribute which this function brings in. The commanding caste tries to strengthen and perpetuate the organs of compulsion. To make sure of its power and income, it spares nothing and nobody. The more the course of development goes against it, the more ruthless it becomes toward the advanced elements of the population. Like the Catholic Church it has put forward the dogma of infallibility in the period of its decline, but it has raised it to a height of which the Roman pope never dreamed.

The increasingly insistent deification of Stalin is, with all its elements of caricature, a necessary element of the regime. The bureaucracy has need of an inviolable super-arbiter, a first consul if not an emperor, and it raises upon its shoulders him who best responds to its claim for lordship. That "strength of character" of the leader which so enraptures the literary dilettantes of the West, is in reality the sum total of the collective pressure of a caste which will stop at nothing in defense of its position. Each one of them at his post is thinking: *l'état — c'est moi.* In Stalin each one easily finds himself. But Stalin also finds in each one a small part of his own spirit. Stalin is the personification of the bureaucracy. That is the substance of his political personality.

Caesarism, or its bourgeois form, Bonapartism, enters the scene in those moments of history when the sharp struggle of two camps raises the state power, so to speak, above the nation, and guarantees it, in appearance, a complete independence of classes — in reality, only the freedom necessary for a defense of the privileged. The Stalin regime, rising above a politically atomized society, resting upon a police and officers' corps, and allowing of no control whatever, is obviously a variation of Bonapartism — a Bonapartism of a new type not before seen in history.

Caesarism arose upon the basis of a slave society shaken by inward strife. Bonapartism is one of the political weapons of the capitalist regime in its critical period.

Stalinism is a variety of the same system, but upon the basis of a workers' state torn by the antagonism between an organized and armed soviet aristocracy and the unarmed toiling masses.

As history testifies, Bonapartism gets along admirably with a universal, and even a secret, ballot. The democratic ritual of Bonapartism is the *plebiscite*. From time to time, the question is presented to the citizens: *for* or *against* the leader? And the voter feels the barrel of a revolver between his shoulders. Since the time of Napoleon III, who now seems a provincial dilettante, this technique has received an extraordinary development. The new Soviet constitution which establishes *Bonapartism on a plebiscite basis* is the veritable crown of the system.

In the last analysis, Soviet Bonapartism owes its birth to the belatedness of the world revolution. But in the capitalist countries the same cause gave rise to fascism. We thus arrive at the conclusion, unexpected at first glance, but in reality inevitable, that the crushing of Soviet democracy by an all-powerful bureaucracy and the extermination of bourgeois democracy by fascism were produced by one and the same cause: the dilatoriness of the world proletariat in solving the problems set for it by history. Stalinism and fascism, in spite of a deep difference in social foundations, are symmetrical phenomena. In many of their features they show a deadly similarity. A victorious revolutionary movement in Europe would immediately shake not only fascism, but Soviet Bonapartism. In turning its back to the international revolution, the Stalinist bureaucracy was, from its own point of view, right. It was merely obeying the voice of self-preservation.

SUGGESTIONS FOR FURTHER READING

The quantity of literature on Soviet Russia and Communism now available in English is staggering. No attempt will be made here to cover it all, but only to suggest to the interested reader some of the most important works dealing with Soviet Russia in general or with particular topics that are especially relevant to the subject of the Stalin Revolution.

The books represented in this selection of readings are all fundamental sources for understanding Soviet Russia and its crucial development in the early 1930's.

For a general view of Soviet history as a whole, there are several good books: Frederick L. Schuman, *Russia Since 1917* (New York, 1957); Georg von Rauch, *A History of Soviet Russia* (London, 1957); Eric Strauss, *Soviet Russia: Anatomy of a Social History* (London, 1939); and the interesting Menshevik interpretation by Raphael Abramovich, *The Soviet Revolution* (New York, 1962). A comprehensive history centering on the Communist Party as an institution is Leonard Schapiro, *The Communist Party of the Soviet Union* (New York, 1960). Julian Steinberg, ed., *Verdict of Three Decades,* (New York, 1950), is a useful collection of critical articles on various stages of Soviet history. The best official Soviet history, long out of print, is N. N. Popov, *Outline History of the Communist Party of the Soviet Union* (2 vols., New York, 1934). A selection of key statements by the Soviet leaders is contained in Robert V. Daniels, ed., *A Documentary History of Communism* (New York, 1960). For a general discussion of Communism in Russia and internationally see Robert V. Daniels, *The Nature of Communism* (New York, 1962).

The best study of the Russian historical and economic background as it relates to the Stalin Revolution is Sir John Maynard, *Russia in Flux* (New York, 1948). Various pertinent historical articles are contained in Ernest J. Simmons, ed., *Continuity and Change in Russian and Soviet Thought* (Cambridge, Mass., 1955) and in Cyril Black, ed., *The Transformation of Russian Society* (Cambridge, Mass., 1960). The more immediate background of revolutionary Russia has been studied exhaustively by E. H. Carr in his *History of Soviet Russia* (6 vols. to date; New York, 1951–).

The political events of the 1920's and '30's are dealt with in detail in Boris Souvarine, *Stalin: A Critical Survey of Bolshevism* (London and New York, 1939) and in Bertram Wolfe, *Khrushchev and Stalin's Ghost* (New York, 1957). (The latter includes the text of Khrushchev's 1956 attack on Stalin and the text of Bukharin's important article of 1928, "Notes of an Economist.") The official hopes were stated by the then Commissar of Finance, G. F. Grinko (later purged), in *The Five-Year Plan of the Soviet Union* (New York, 1930), while the claims of progress were recorded in collected speeches of the top Soviet leaders — J. V. Stalin et al., *From the First to the Second Five-Year Plan* (New York, 1934), and *Socialism Victorious* (New York, 1935). An inside view of Soviet politics during the Stalin Revolution is afforded by the one-time Communist Party official Abdurakhman Avtorkhanov, in *Stalin and the Soviet Communist Party* (New York, 1959).

There are many journalistic and autobiographical accounts of the Stalin Revolution; representative books by correspondents are William Henry Chamberlin, *Russia's Iron Age* (Boston, 1937), Maurice Hindus, *Humanity Uprooted* (New York,

1930), and Hindus, *Red Bread* (New York, 1931); John Scott's *Behind the Urals* (Boston, 1943) is the account of an American who worked in the Soviet steel industry; and Victor Kravchenko, *I Chose Freedom* (New York, 1946), is the personal account (apparently somewhat fictionalized) of a Soviet engineer who later defected to the West.

The background of socialist and Communist theory is ably presented in Carl Landauer, *European Socialism* (2 vols., Berkeley, California, 1959) and in John Plamenatz, *German Marxism and Russian Communism* (London, New York, 1954). The present official interpretation of Marxism-Leninism is expounded in O. V. Kuusinen, et al., *Fundamentals of Marxism-Leninism* (Moscow, 1961). Certain theoretical implications of the Stalin Revolution are pursued in Robert V. Daniels, "Towards a Definition of Soviet Socialism," *New Politics,* Vol. I, no. 4 (1962), pp. 111–118.

The development of the Soviet government before, during, and after the Stalin Revolution is treated in many texts, one of the best of which is Merle Fainsod, *How Russia Is Ruled* (Cambridge, Mass., 1953). W. W. Kulski, *The Soviet Regime* (Syracuse, 1954; third revised and condensed edition, 1959) is good on the political, economic, and legal institutions which emerged from the Stalin Revolution, and their impact on the Soviet citizen. A lengthy and favorable analysis of the Soviet system is contained in Sidney and Beatrice Webb, *Soviet Communism: A New Civilization?* (2 vols., London, 1935). Soviet totalitarianism is analyzed in Carl J. Friedrich and Zbigniew Brzezinski, *Totalitarian Dictatorship and Autocracy* (Cambridge, Mass., 1956), while the events of the purges that followed the Stalin Revolution are analyzed in Brzezinski, *The Permanent Purge* (Cambridge, Mass., 1956).

The economic side of the Stalin Revolution and of Soviet Russia generally has been subjected to more careful analysis than any other aspect of these events. The principles of the Soviet economy are ably analyzed in Robert W. Campbell, *Soviet Economic Power* (Cambridge, Mass., 1960), while the main economic institutions and problems are described in Harry Schwartz, *Russia's Soviet Economy* (New York, 1950). Maurice Dobb, *Soviet Economic Development since 1917* (New York, 1948) is a favorable but useful history. Naum Jasny, *Soviet Industrialization* (New York, 1961), analyzes the economic plans and performance since 1928. The organization and problems of industry are treated in Joseph S. Berliner, *Factory and Manager in the USSR* (Cambridge, Mass., 1957), and in David Granick, *The Red Executive* (Garden City, New York, 1961). Solomon Schwartz, *Labor in the Soviet Union* (New York, 1952), covers the history of labor conditions and organization. Ellsworth Raymond, *Soviet Economic Progress: Because of or in Spite of the Government?* (New York, 1957), is a useful collection of readings representing various judgments.

Two important books on the social policies of Stalin's government are Nicholas Timasheff, *The Great Retreat* (New York, 1946), and Max Eastman, *Stalin's Russia and the Crisis in Socialism* (New York, 1940). See also Robert V. Daniels, "Soviet Thought in the 1930's," Indiana Slavic Studies, I (1956), pp. 97–135. Particular areas of social and cultural policy have been treated in a series of good works in addition to those represented in the present volume: on law, Harold Berman, *Justice in Russia* (Cambridge, Mass., 1950); on religion, John S. Curtiss, *The Russian Church and the Soviet State* (Boston, 1953); on national attitudes and the minorities, Frederick Barghoorn, *Soviet Russian Nationalism* (New York, 1956); on philosophy and Marxist doctrine, Gustavo Wetter, *Dialectical Materialism* (New York, 1958) and Klaus Mehnert, *Stalin vs. Marx* (London, 1952); on history writing, Konstantin

F. Shteppa, *Russian Historians and the Soviet State* (New Brunswick, New Jersey, 1962); on literature, Gleb Struve, *Soviet Russian Literature 1917–1950* (Norman, Oklahoma, 1951). A variety of good articles are brought together in Alex Inkeles and Kent Geiger, eds., *Soviet Society: A Book of Readings* (Boston, 1961).